100 BEST LOVED PIANO SOLOS
VOLUME 1

Arranged by
Robert Schultz

CONTENTS

POPULAR HITS

MOVIE & TV MUSIC

POP, ROCK & COUNTRY CLASSICS

FOLK & CHILDREN'S SONGS

CLASSICAL THEMES

ALL-TIME FAVORITES

From the Motion Picture "THE PREACHER'S WIFE"

I BELIEVE IN YOU AND ME

Words and Music by
SANDY LINZER and DAVID WOLFERT
Arranged by ROBERT SCHULTZ

Moderately slow

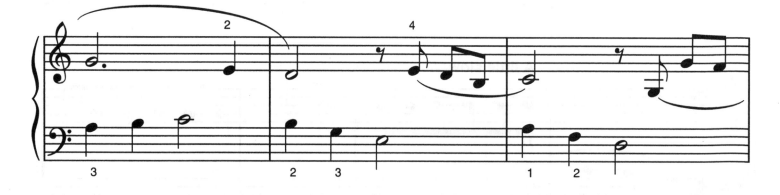

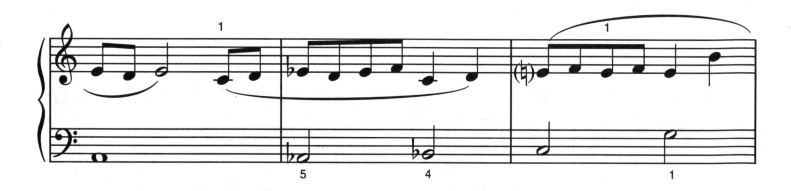

I Believe in You and Me - 2 - 1
AS006

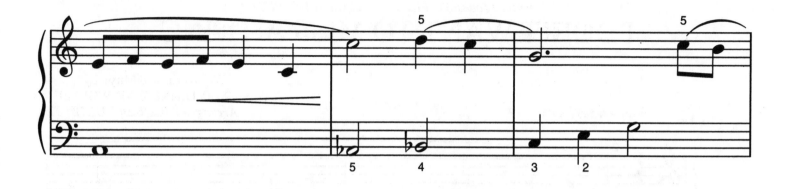

From Touchstone Pictures' "ARMAGEDDON"

I DON'T WANT TO MISS A THING

Words and Music by
DIANE WARREN
Arranged by ROBERT SCHULTZ

Moderately

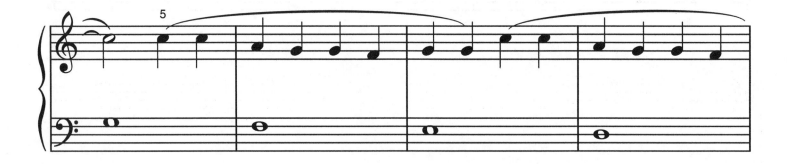

I Don't Want to Miss a Thing - 2 - 1
AS006

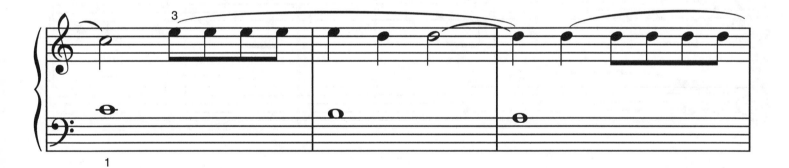

I LOVE THE WAY YOU LOVE ME

Words and Music by
VICTORIA SHAW and
CHUCK CANNON
Arranged by ROBERT SCHULTZ

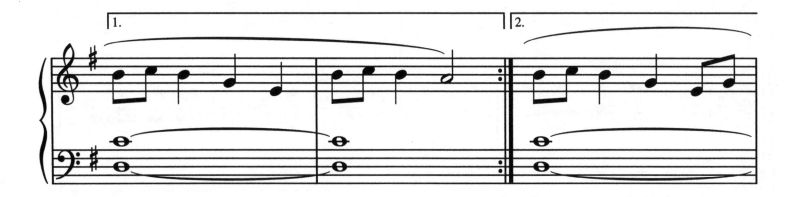

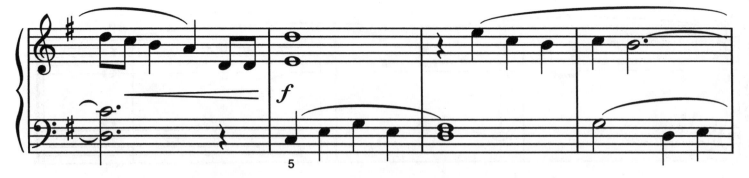

I Love the Way You Love Me - 2 - 1
AS006

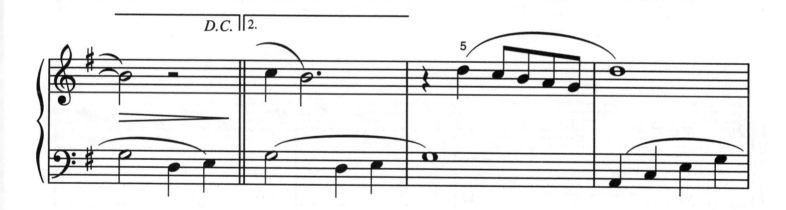

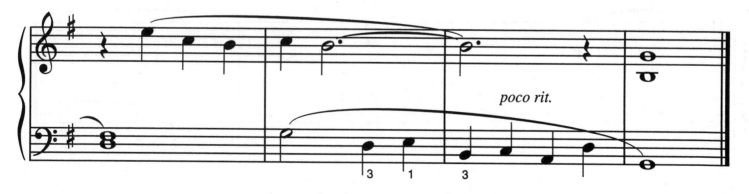

I Love the Way You Love Me - 2 - 2

I STILL BELIEVE IN YOU

Words and Music by
VINCE GILL and JOHN BARLOW JARVIS
Arranged by ROBERT SCHULTZ

Moderately slow

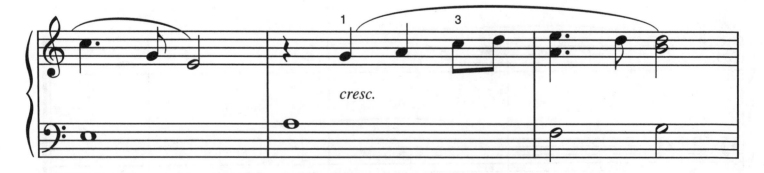

I Still Believe in You - 2 - 1
AS006

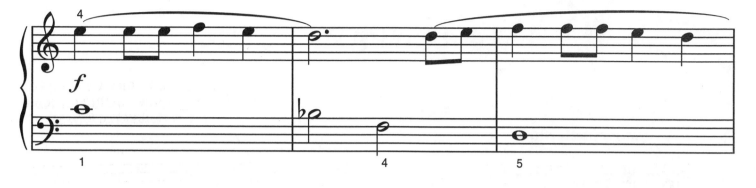

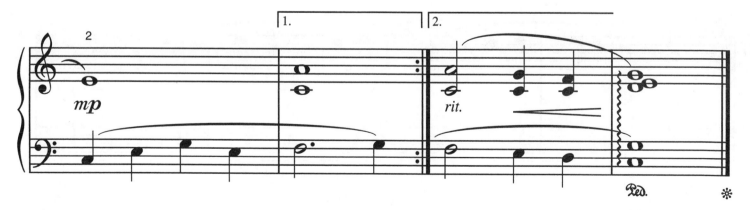

I Still Believe in You - 2 - 2

I SWEAR

Words and Music by
GARY BAKER and FRANK MYERS
Arranged by ROBERT SCHULTZ

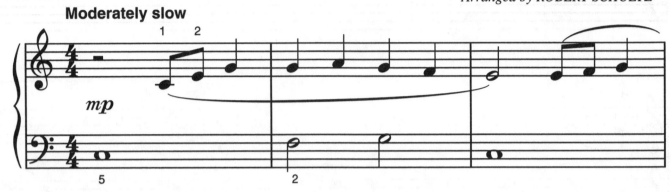

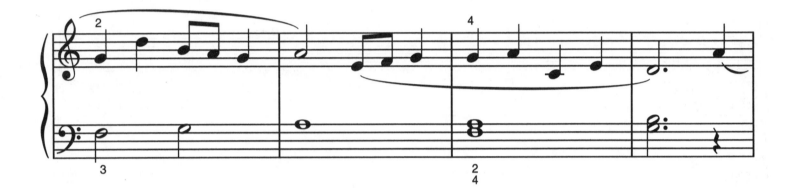

I Swear - 2 - 1
AS006

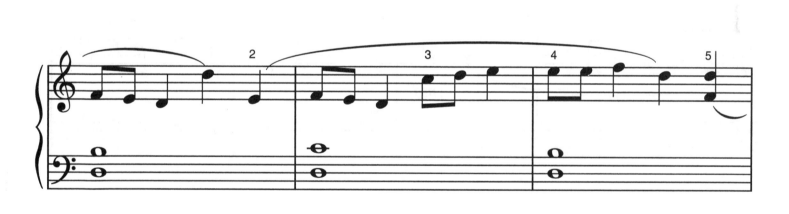

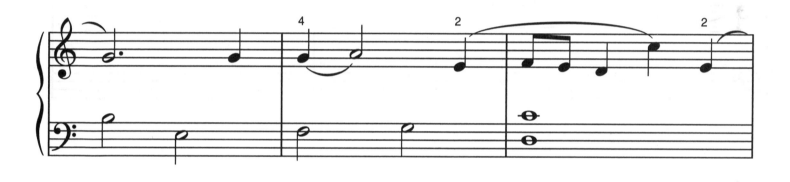

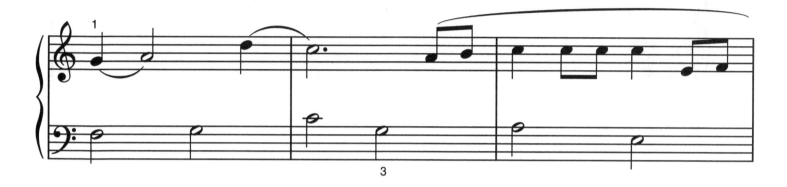

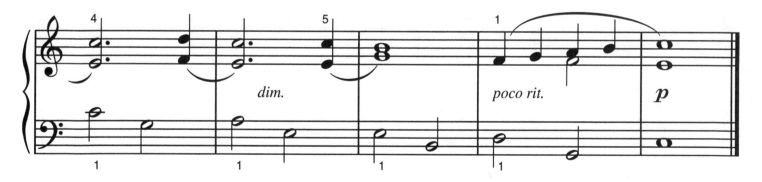

IF WE WERE LOVERS

Words and Music by
GLORIA ESTEFAN & EMILIO ESTEFAN, JR.
Arranged by ROBERT SCHULTZ

Easily ♩ = 88

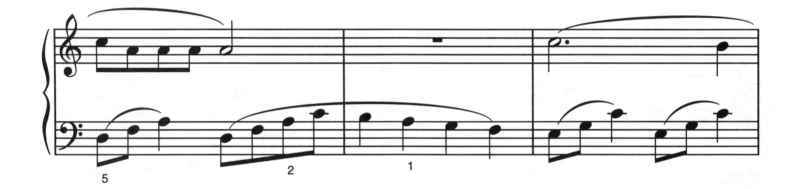

If We Were Lovers - 4 - 1
AS006

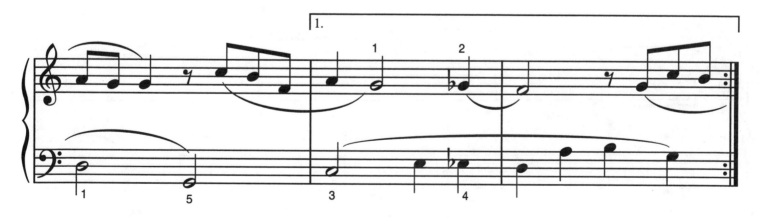

If We Were Lovers - 4 - 2

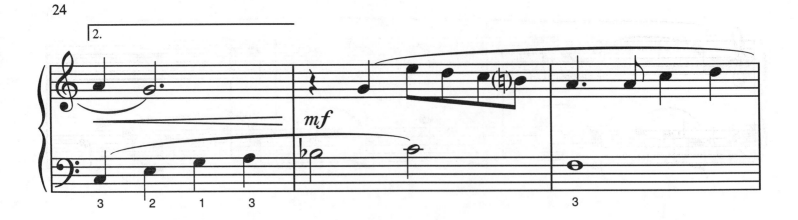

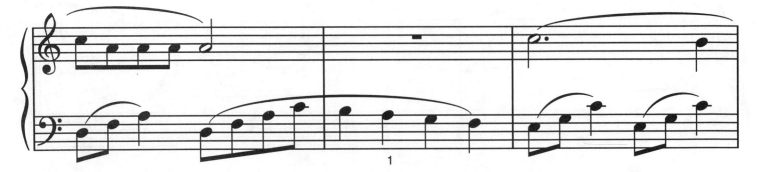

poco rit.

p

If We Were Lovers - 4 - 4

I'M FREE

Words and Music by
JON SECADA and MIGUEL A. MOREJON
Arranged by ROBERT SCHULTZ

Moderately ♩ = 100

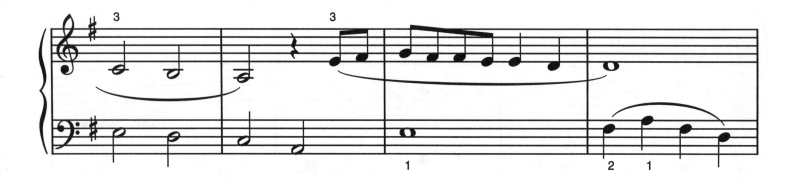

I'm Free - 2 - 1
AS006

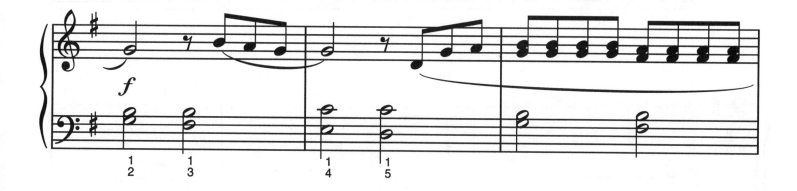

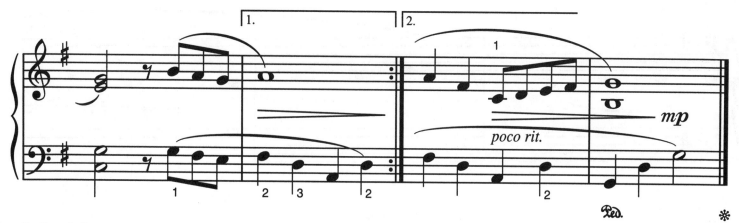

I'm Free - 2 - 2

MORE THAN WORDS

Lyrics and Music by
BETTENCOURT and CHERONE
Arranged by ROBERT SCHULTZ

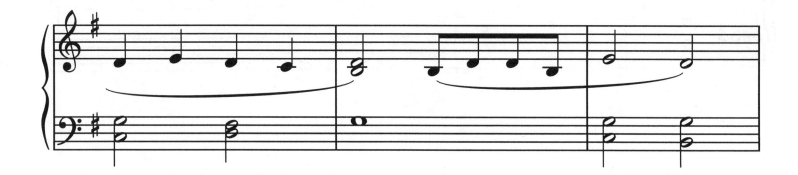

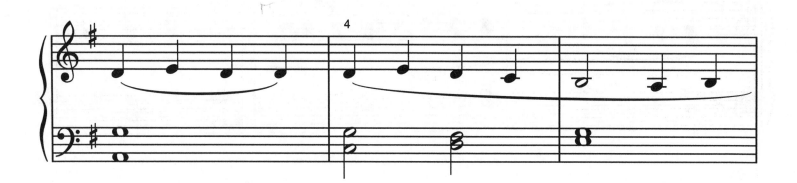

More Than Words - 2 - 1
AS006

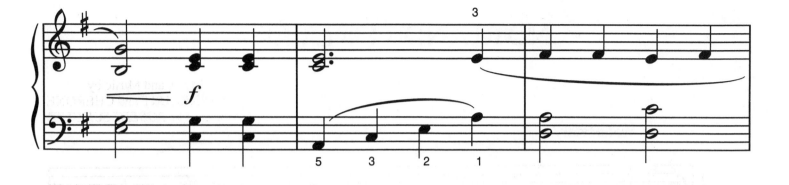

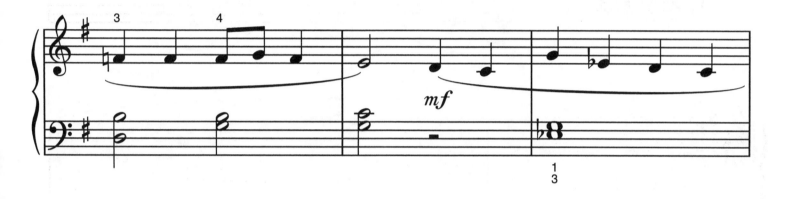

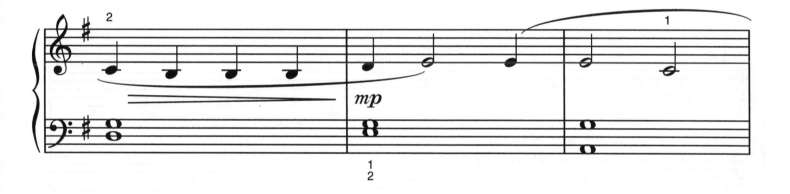

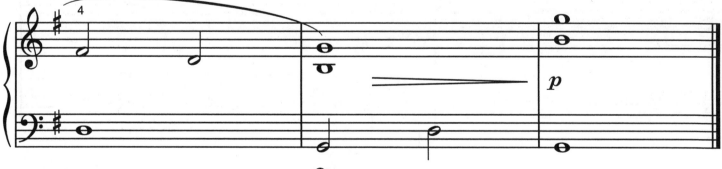

More Than Words - 2 - 2

NOW AND FOREVER

Music and Lyrics by
RICHARD MARX
Arranged by ROBERT SCHULTZ

Moderately slow

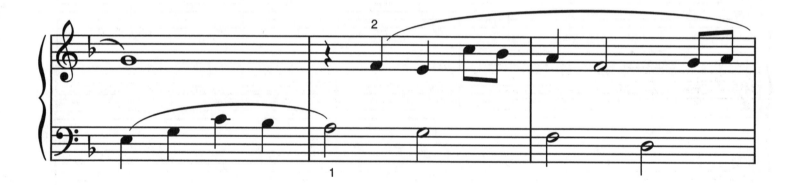

Now and Forever - 2 - 1
AS006

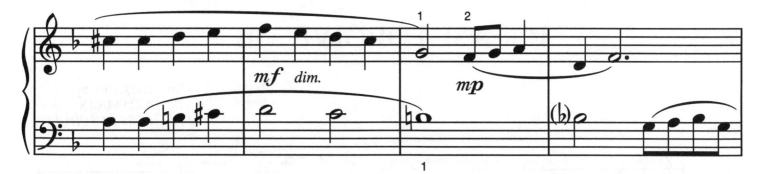

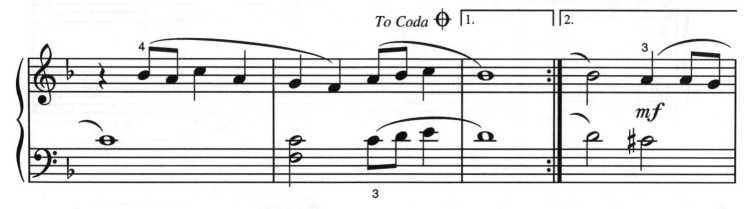

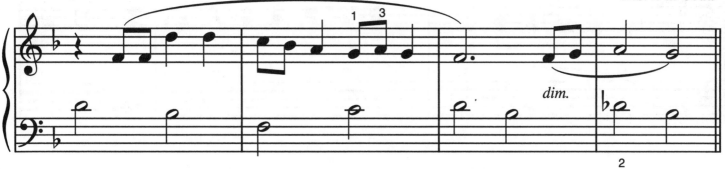

PLEASE FORGIVE ME

Words and Music by BRYAN ADAMS
and ROBERT JOHN "MUTT" LANGE
Arranged by ROBERT SCHULTZ

Please Forgive Me - 3 - 1
AS006

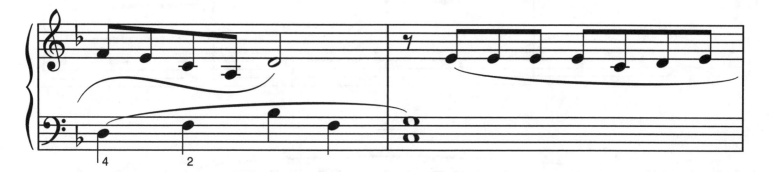

34

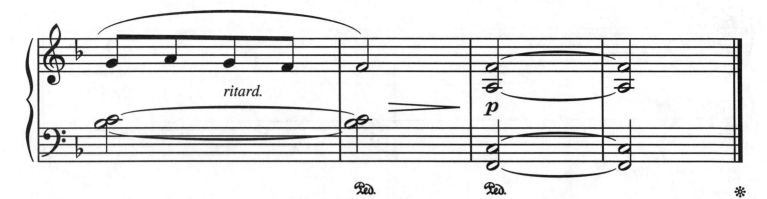

From the Original Motion Picture Soundtrack "BEACHES"

THE WIND BENEATH MY WINGS

Words and Music by
LARRY HENLEY and JEFF SILBAR
Arranged by ROBERT SCHULTZ

Gently, flowing

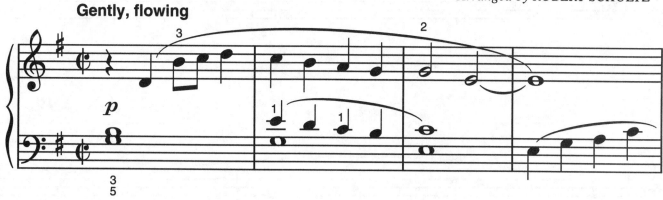

The Wind beneath My Wings - 3 - 1
AS006

36

The Wind beneath My Wings - 3 - 2

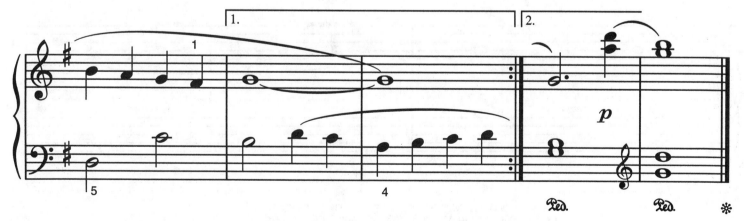

The Wind beneath My Wings - 3 - 3

SAID I LOVED YOU . . . BUT I LIED

Composed by MICHAEL BOLTON
and ROBERT JOHN "MUTT" LANGE
Arranged by ROBERT SCHULTZ

Slowly ♩ = 88

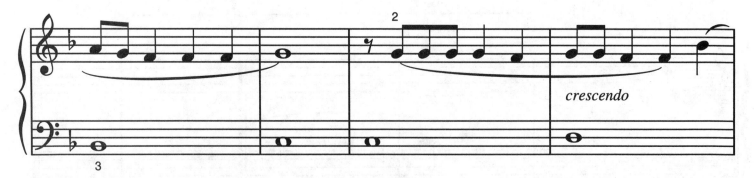

crescendo

Said I Loved You . . . But I Lied - 2 - 1
AS006

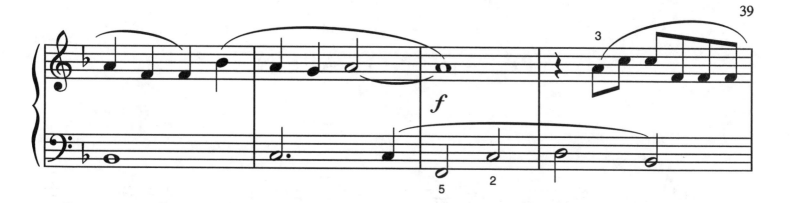

YOU ARE NOT ALONE

Written and Composed by
R. KELLY
Arranged by ROBERT SCHULTZ

You Are Not Alone - 2 - 1
AS006

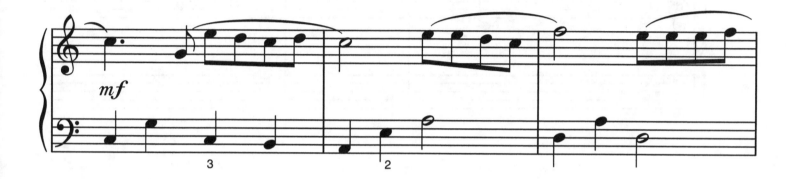

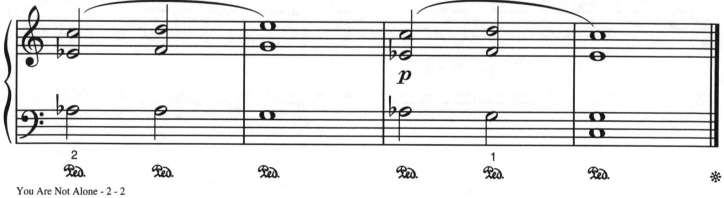

YOU'RE THE INSPIRATION

Words and Music by
DAVID FOSTER and
PETER CETERA
Arranged by ROBERT SCHULTZ

Moderately slow

You're the Inspiration - 2 - 1
AS006

A Greenway Production in Association with 20th Century-Fox TV for ABC-TV

BATMAN THEME

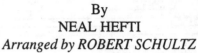

By
NEAL HEFTI
Arranged by ROBERT SCHULTZ

Bat rock tempo

JEOPARDY THEME

Music by
MERV GRIFFIN
Arranged by ROBERT SCHULTZ

Thoughtfully

CHARLIE BROWN THEME

By VINCE GUARALDI
Arranged by ROBERT SCHULTZ

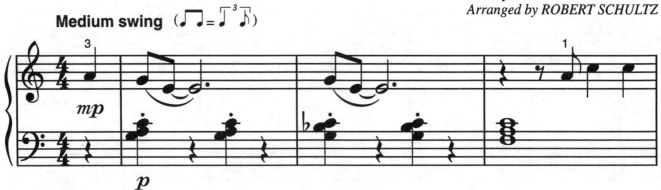

Charlie Brown Theme - 2 - 1
AS006

Charlie Brown Theme - 2 - 2

From the TV Show "PEANUTS SPECIAL"

LINUS AND LUCY

By VINCE GUARALDI
Arranged by ROBERT SCHULTZ

Moderately

Linus and Lucy - 2 - 1
AS006

Linus and Lucy - 2 - 2

From the Warner Bros. Picture "DAYS OF WINE AND ROSES"

DAYS OF WINE AND ROSES

Lyric by
JOHNNY MERCER

Music by
HENRY MANCINI
Arranged by ROBERT SCHULTZ

Moderately

Days of Wine and Roses - 2 - 1
AS006

Days of Wine and Roses - 2 - 2

From the MGM/UA Motion Picture "THE SECRET OF NIMH"

FLYING DREAMS

Lyrics by PAUL WILLIAMS

Music by JERRY GOLDSMITH
Arranged by ROBERT SCHULTZ

Gentle waltz

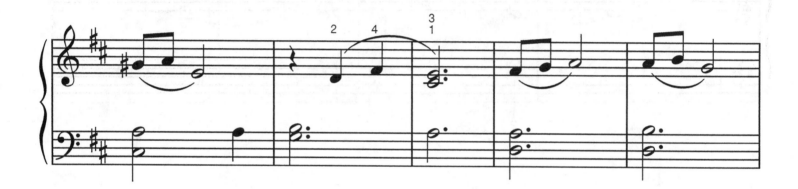

Flying Dreams - 2 - 1
AS006

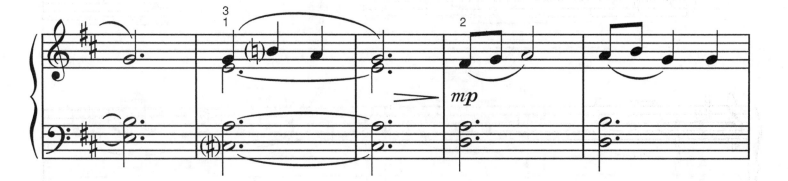

I'LL BE THERE FOR YOU
(Theme from "Friends")

Words by
DAVID CRANE, MARTA KAUFFMAN, ALLEE WILLIS,
PHIL SOLEM and DANNY WILDE

Music by
MICHAEL SKLOFF
Arranged by ROBERT SCHULTZ

Fast rock ♩ = 92

I'll Be There for You - 2 - 1
AS006

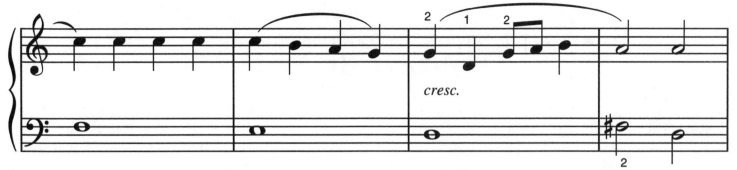

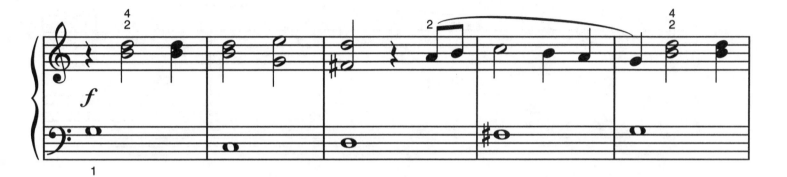

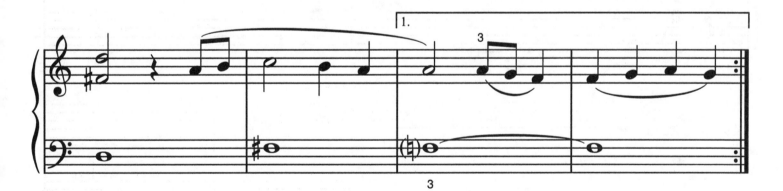

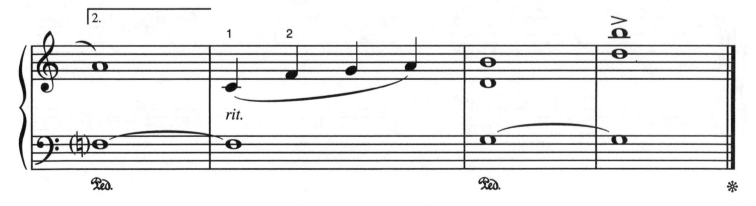

Columbia Pictures Presents a Mirage/Punch Production: a Sidney Pollack Film "TOOTSIE"

IT MIGHT BE YOU
(Theme from "Tootsie")

Words by
ALAN and MARILYN BERGMAN

Music by
DAVE GRUSIN
Arranged by ROBERT SCHULTZ

Moderately

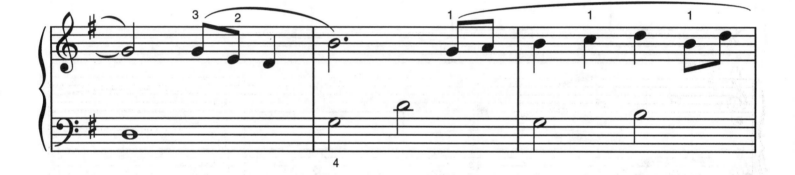

It Might Be You - 2 - 1
AS006

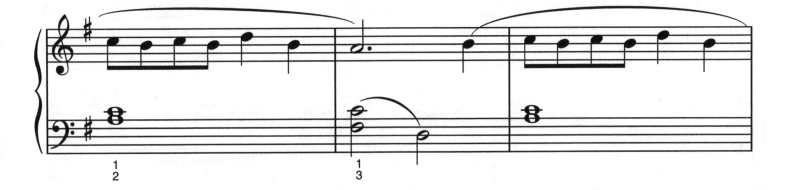

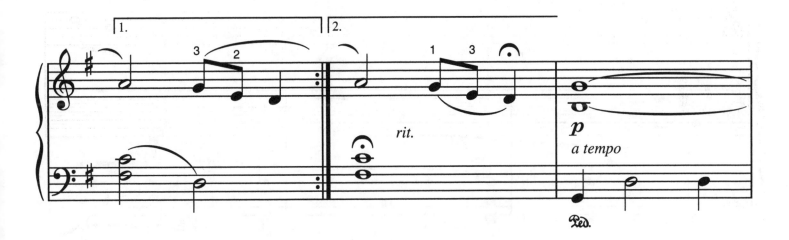

It Might Be You - 2 - 2

Theme Song from the Mirisch-G&E Production, "THE PINK PANTHER," a United Artists Release

THE PINK PANTHER

Music by HENRY MANCINI
Arranged by ROBERT SCHULTZ

Mysteriously

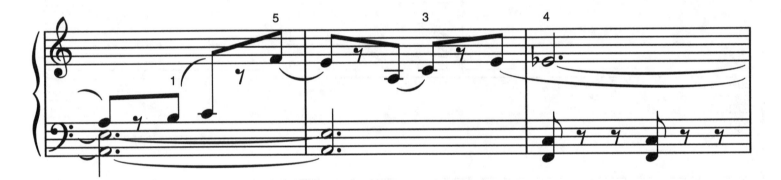

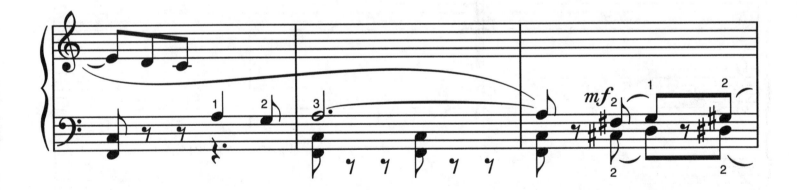

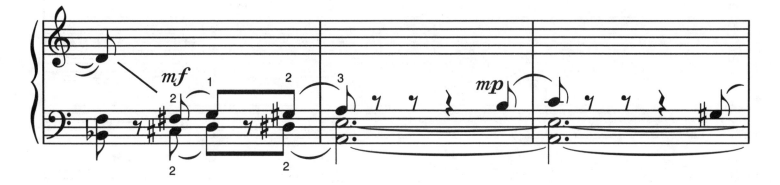

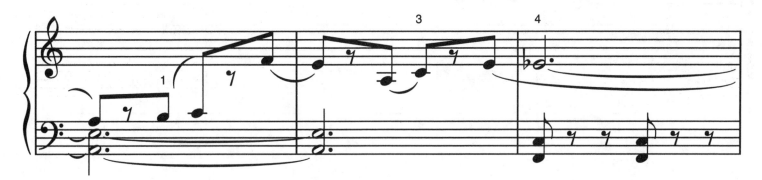

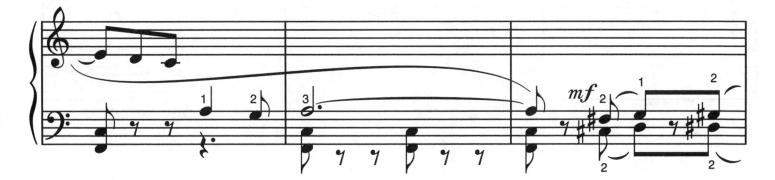

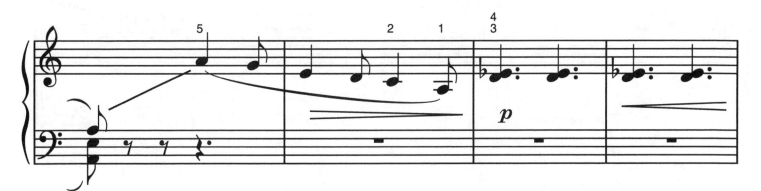

60

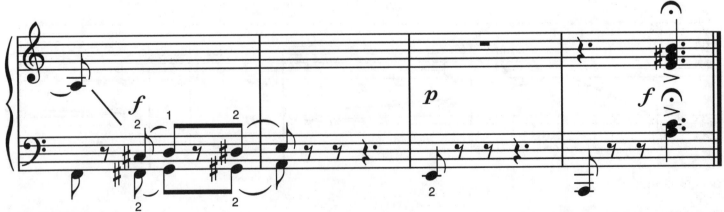

The Pink Panther - 3 - 3

Metro-Goldwyn-Mayer Presents David Lean's Film "DOCTOR ZHIVAGO"

LARA'S THEME FROM "DOCTOR ZHIVAGO"

(Somewhere, My Love)

Music by
MAURICE JARRE
Arranged by ROBERT SCHULTZ

Very flowing, not too slow

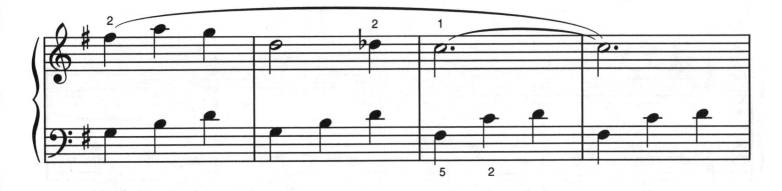

Lara's Theme from "Doctor Zhivago" - 3 - 1
AS006

62

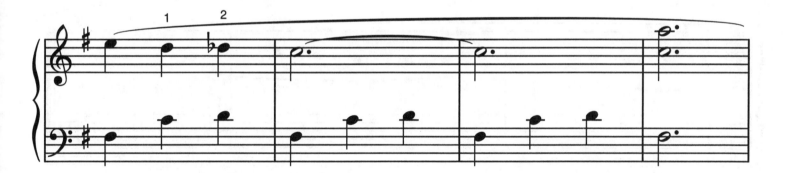

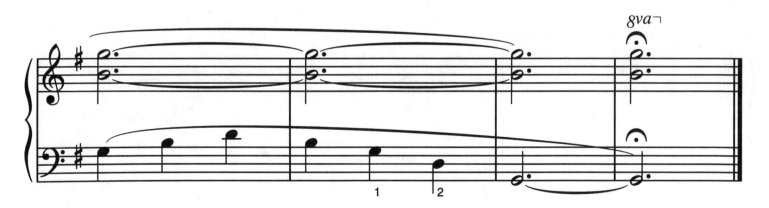

Lara's Theme from "Doctor Zhivago" - 3 - 3

From Warner Bros. "QUEST FOR CAMELOT"

LOOKING THROUGH YOUR EYES

Words and Music by
CAROLE BAYER SAGER
and DAVID FOSTER
Arranged by ROBERT SCHULTZ

Moderately

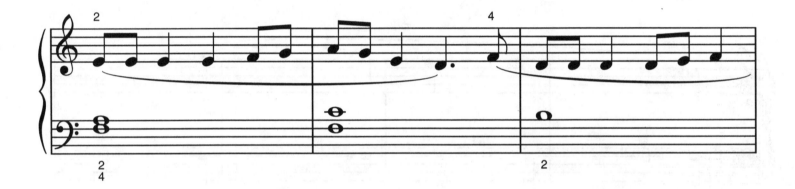

Looking Through Your Eyes - 2 - 1
AS006

Columbia Pictures Presents a Channel-Lauren Shuler Production
A Joel Schumacher Film "ST. ELMO'S FIRE"

LOVE THEME FROM ST. ELMO'S FIRE

(Instrumental)

By DAVID FOSTER
Arranged by ROBERT SCHULTZ

Moderately

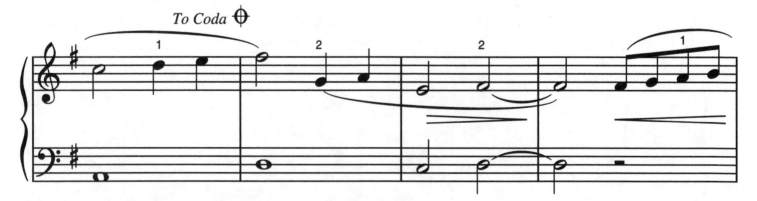

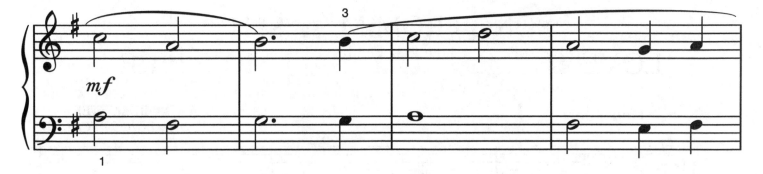

D.C. al Coda

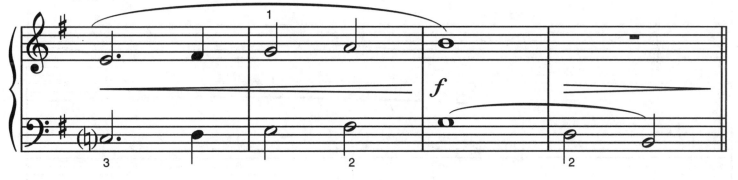

Love Theme from St. Elmo's Fire - 2 - 2

SONG FROM M*A*S*H
(Suicide Is Painless)

Words and Music by
MIKE ALTMAN and JOHNNY MANDEL
Arranged by ROBERT SCHULTZ

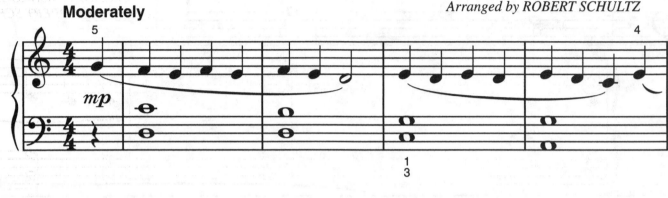

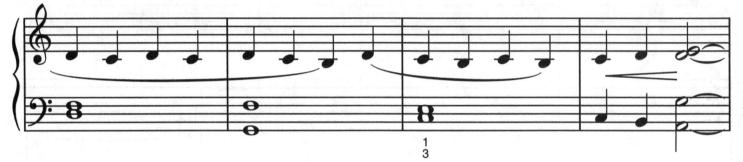

From the Twentieth Century-Fox Motion Picture "THE ROSE"

THE ROSE

Words and Music by
AMANDA McBROOM
Arranged by ROBERT SCHULTZ

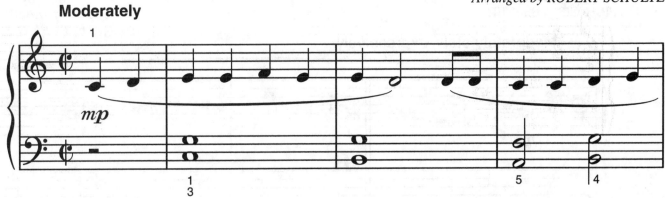

From the 20th Century-Fox Motion Picture "THE SANDPIPER"

THE SHADOW OF YOUR SMILE
(Love Theme from "The Sandpiper")

Lyric by
PAUL FRANCIS WEBSTER

Music by
JOHNNY MANDEL
Arranged by ROBERT SCHULTZ

Moderately slow, expressively

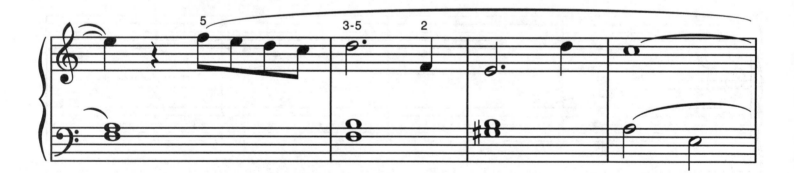

The Shadow of Your Smile - 2 - 1
AS006

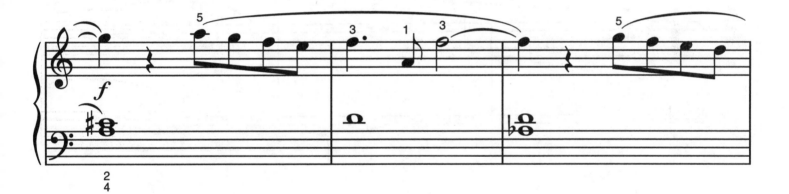

From the Lucasfilm Ltd. Production - A Twentieth Century-Fox Release "STAR WARS"

STAR WARS
(Main Title)

Music by
JOHN WILLIAMS
Arranged by ROBERT SCHULTZ

Boldly

Star Wars (Main Title) - 2 - 1
AS006

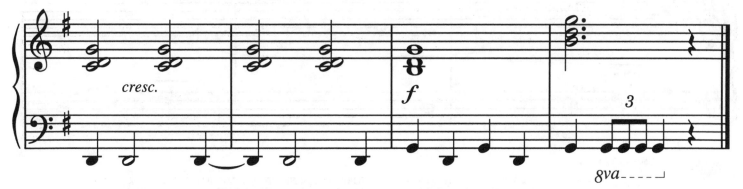

Star Wars (Main Title) - 2 - 2

From the Columbia Picture "ICE CASTLES"

THEME FROM ICE CASTLES

(Through the Eyes of Love)

Lyrics by
CAROLE BAYER SAGER

Music by
MARVIN HAMLISCH
Arranged by ROBERT SCHULTZ

Moderately

Theme from Ice Castles - 2 - 1
AS006

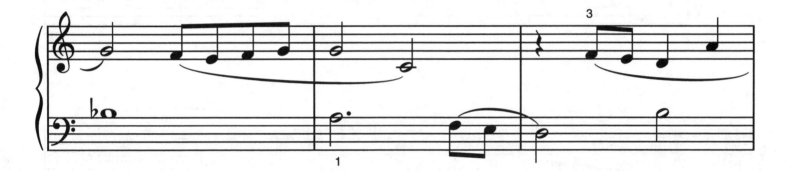

Theme from Ice Castles - 2 - 2

Theme Song from the Stanley Donen Production, a 20th Century-Fox Film

TWO FOR THE ROAD

Words by
LESLIE BRICUSSE

Music by
HENRY MANCINI
Arranged by ROBERT SCHULTZ

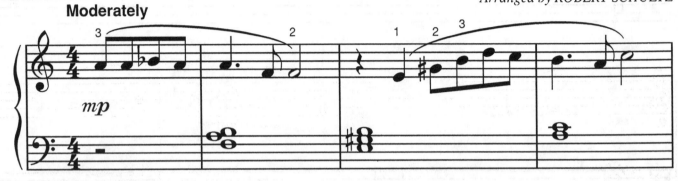

Two for the Road - 2 - 1
AS006

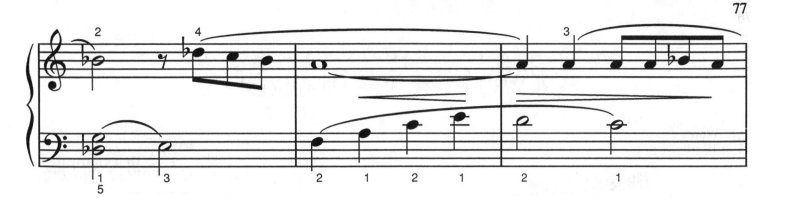

Two for the Road - 2 - 2

From the Motion Picture "AN OFFICER AND A GENTLEMAN"

UP WHERE WE BELONG

Words by
WILL JENNINGS

Music by
JACK NITZSCHE
and BUFFY SAINTE-MARIE
Arranged by ROBERT SCHULTZ

Moderately slow

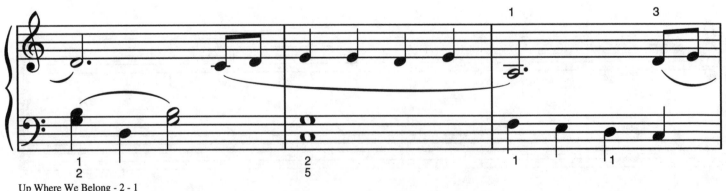

Up Where We Belong - 2 - 1
AS006

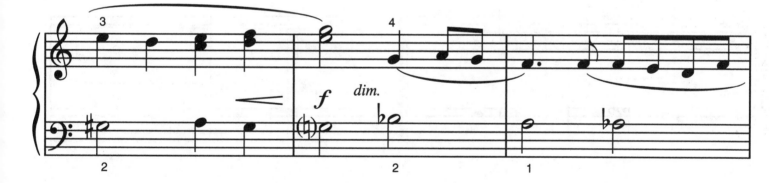

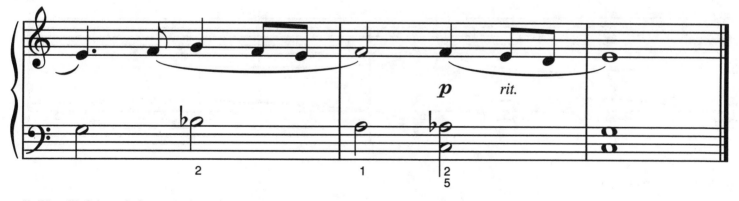

Up Where We Belong - 2 - 2

From the Tristar Pictures Feature Film "HOOK"

WE DON'T WANNA GROW UP

By LESLIE BRICUSSE
and JOHN WILLIAMS
Arranged by ROBERT SCHULTZ

Maturely

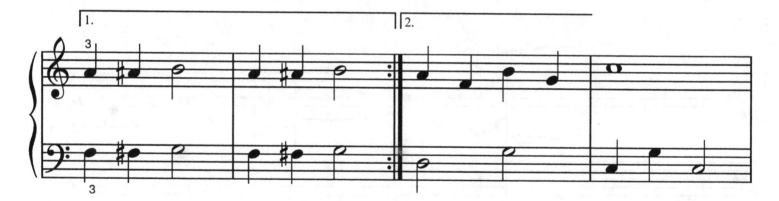

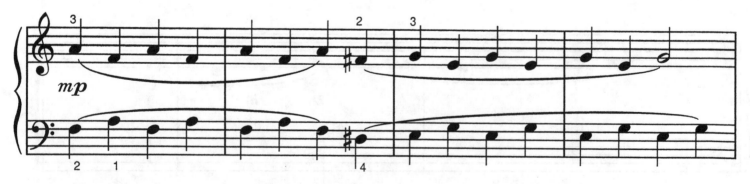

We Don't Wanna Grow Up - 2 - 1
AS006

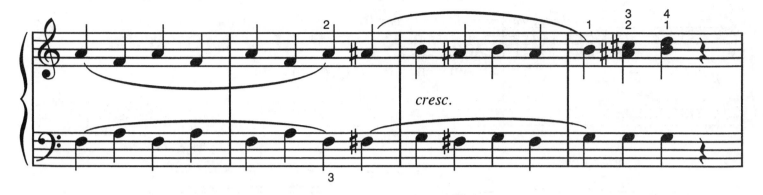

We Don't Wanna Grow Up - 2 - 2

From the United Artists Motion Picture "THE THOMAS CROWN AFFAIR"

THE WINDMILLS OF YOUR MIND

(Theme From "The Thomas Crown Affair")

Lyric by
ALAN and MARILYN BERGMAN

Music by
MICHEL LEGRAND
Arranged by ROBERT SCHULTZ

The Windmills of Your Mind - 2 - 1
AS006

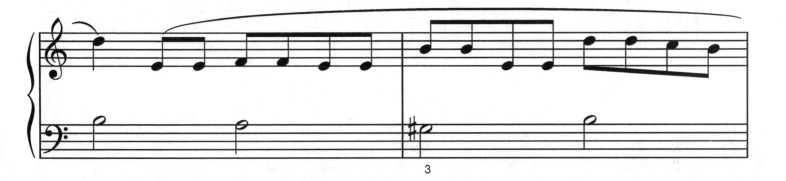

The Windmills of Your Mind - 2 - 2

83

From the Columbia Pictures Release "YOU LIGHT UP MY LIFE"

YOU LIGHT UP MY LIFE

Words and Music by
JOE BROOKS
Arranged by ROBERT SCHULTZ

Moderately

You Light up My Life - 2 - 1
AS006

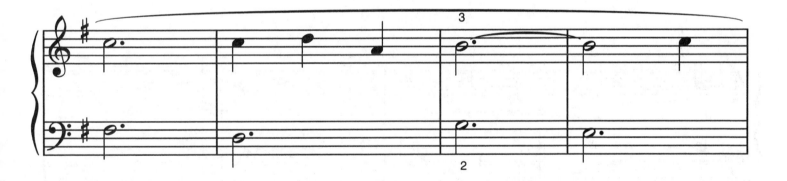

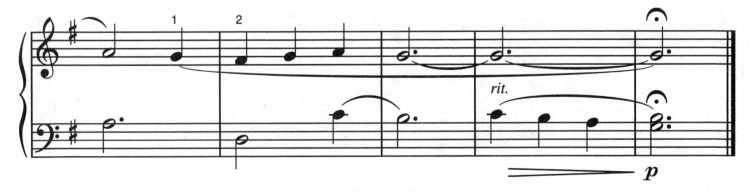

You Light up My Life - 2 - 2

20th Century-Fox Presents an Arthur P. Jacobs Production "DOCTOR DOLITTLE"

TALK TO THE ANIMALS

Words and Music by
LESLIE BRICUSSE
Arranged by ROBERT SCHULTZ

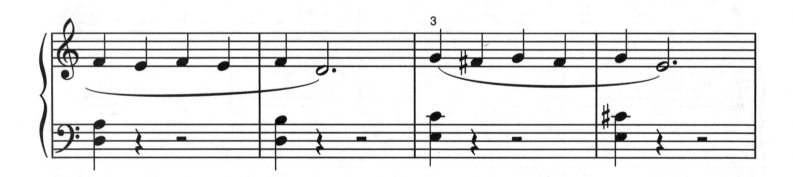

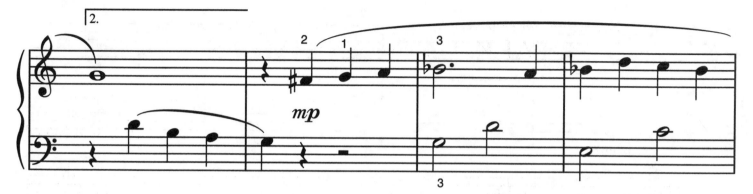

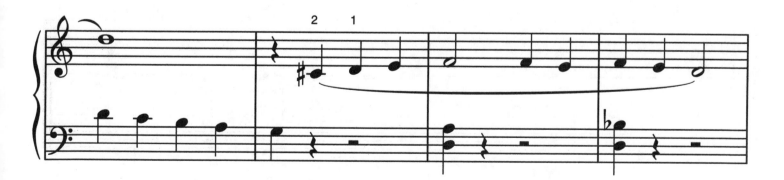

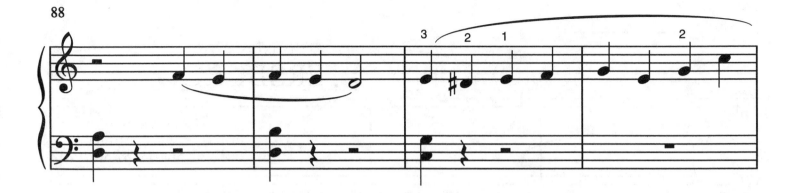

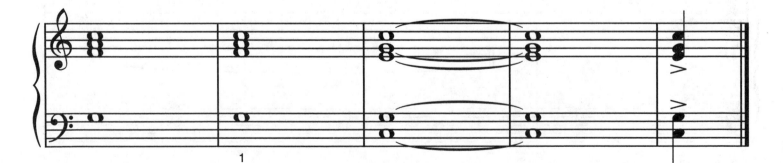

From the Twentieth Century Fox Motion Picture "ANASTASIA"

A RUMOR IN ST. PETERSBURG

Lyrics by
LYNN AHRENS

Music by
STEPHEN FLAHERTY
Arranged by ROBERT SCHULTZ

Moderately fast

A Rumor in St. Petersburg - 5 - 1
AS006

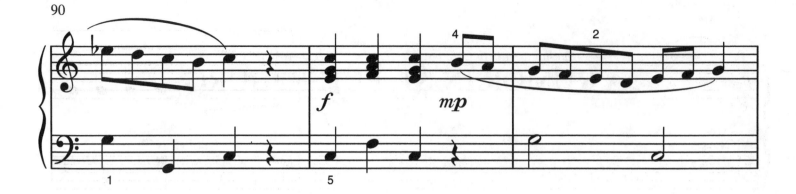

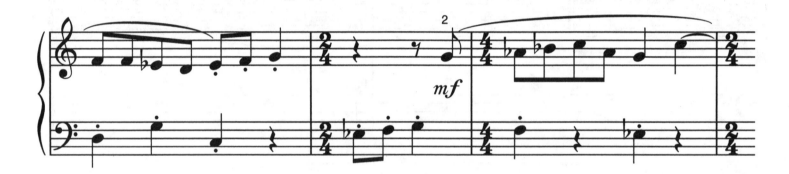

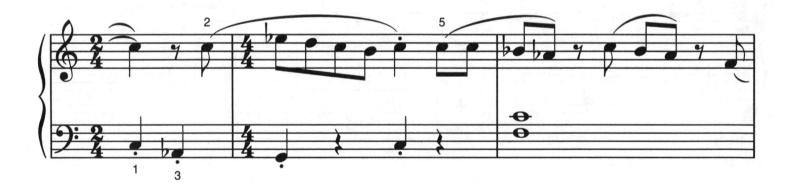

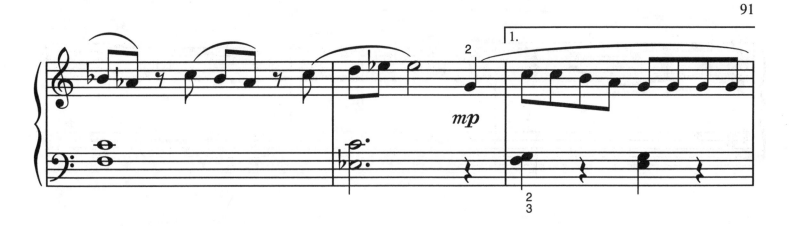

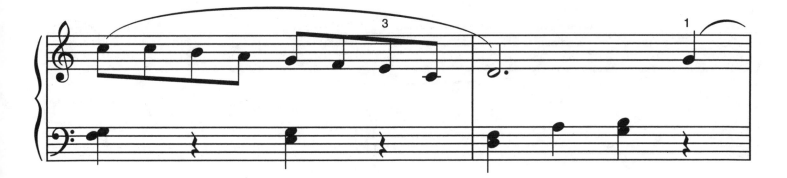

A Rumor in St. Petersburg - 5 - 3

92

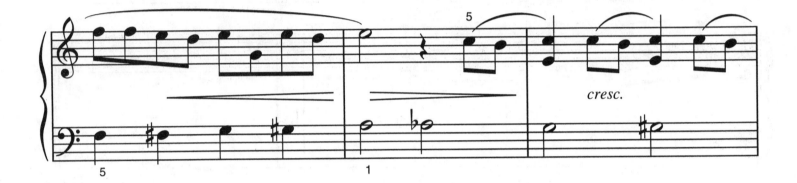

A Rumor in St. Petersburg - 5 - 4

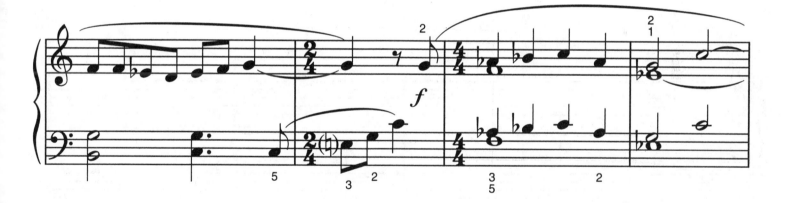

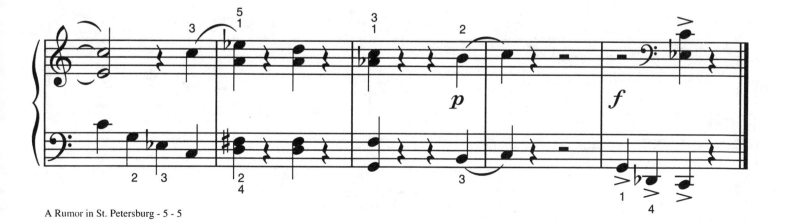

A Rumor in St. Petersburg - 5 - 5

From the Twentieth Century Fox Motion Picture "ANASTASIA"

JOURNEY TO THE PAST

Lyrics by
LYNN AHRENS

Music by
STEPHEN FLAHERTY
Arranged by ROBERT SCHULTZ

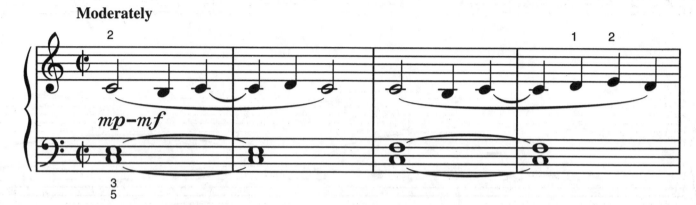

Journey to the Past - 4 - 1
AS006

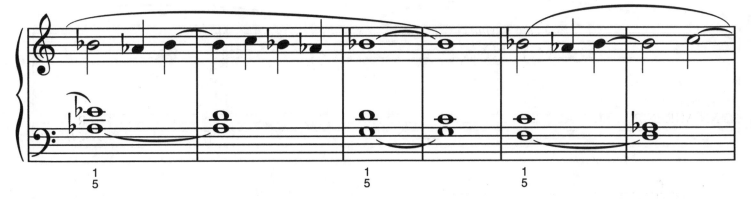

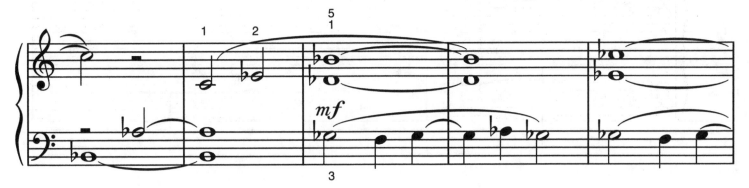

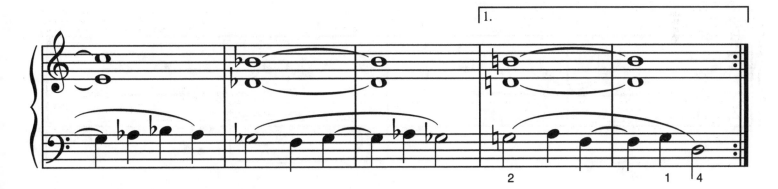

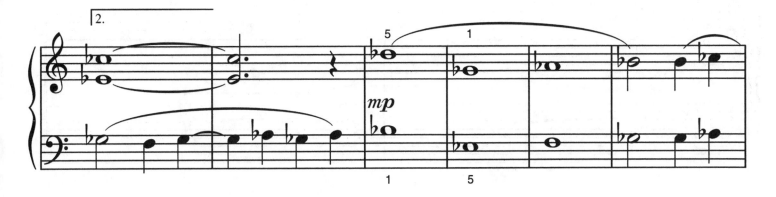

Journey to the Past - 4 - 2

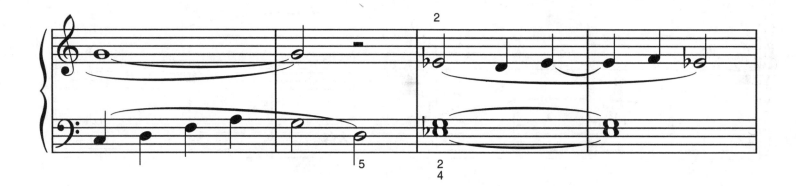

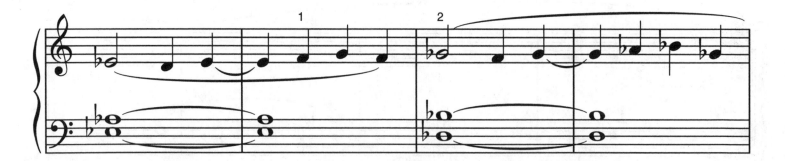

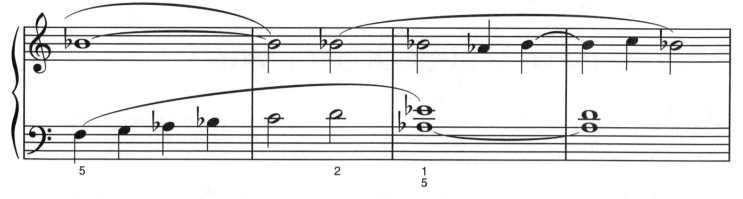

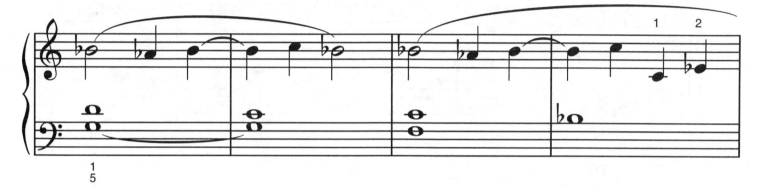

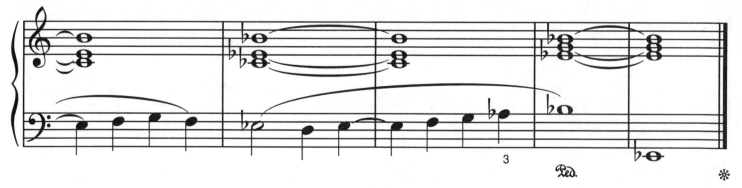

Journey to the Past - 4 - 4

From the Twentieth Century Fox Motion Picture "ANASTASIA"

ONCE UPON A DECEMBER

Lyrics by
LYNN AHRENS

Music by
STEPHEN FLAHERTY
Arranged by ROBERT SCHULTZ

Moderate waltz

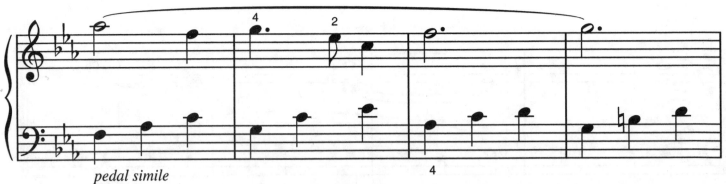

Once Upon a December - 4 - 1
AS006

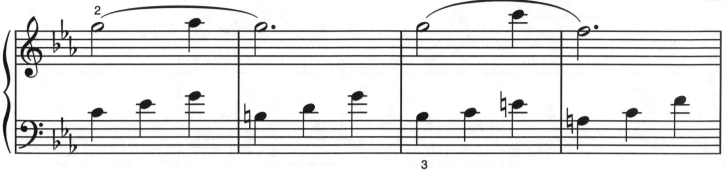

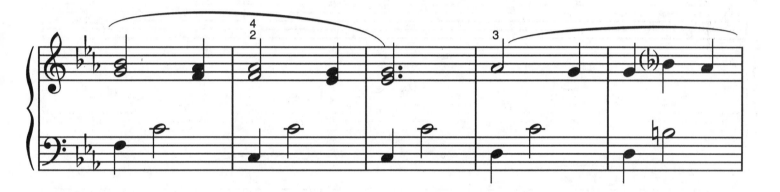

Once Upon a December - 4 - 2

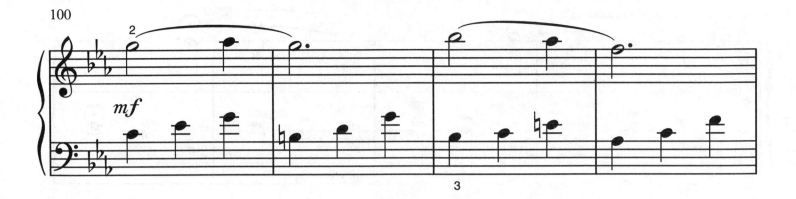

A little slower

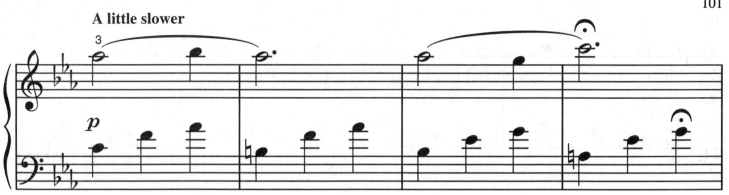

poco rit.

a tempo

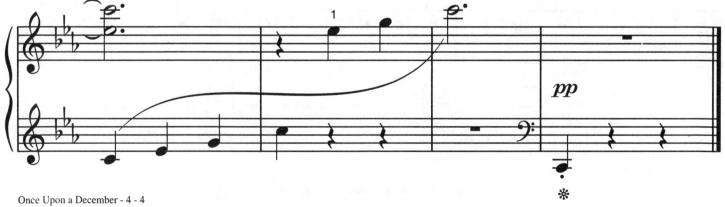

pp

Once Upon a December - 4 - 4

From the Twentieth Century Fox Motion Picture "ANASTASIA"

LEARN TO DO IT

Lyrics by
LYNN AHRENS

Music by
STEPHEN FLAHERTY
Arranged by ROBERT SCHULTZ

Learn to Do It - 6 - 1
AS006

Learn to Do It - 6 - 2

104

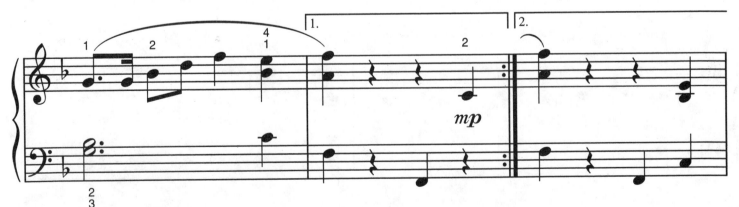

Learn to Do It - 6 - 4

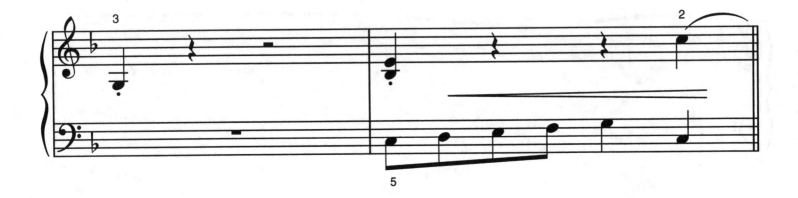

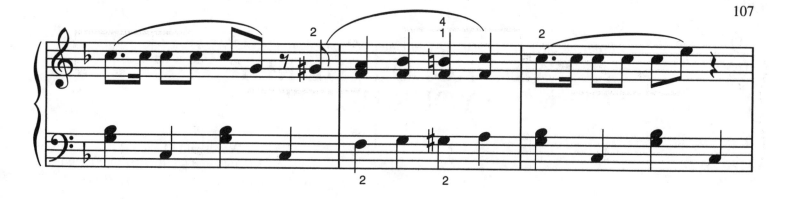

Learn to Do It - 6 - 6

8va.

From the Twentieth Century Fox Animated Motion Picture "ANASTASIA"

PARIS HOLDS THE KEY
(TO YOUR HEART)

Words and Music by
LYNN AHRENS and STEPHEN FLAHERTY
Arranged by ROBERT SCHULTZ

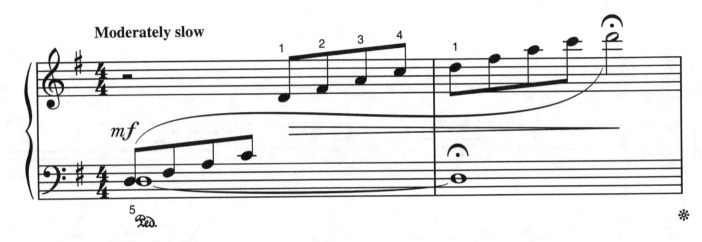

Paris Holds the Key (To Your Heart) - 4 - 1
AS006

109

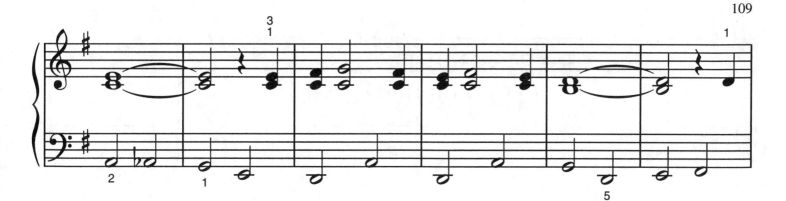

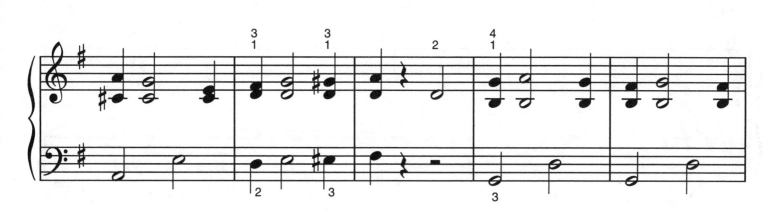

To Coda ⊕

Paris Holds the Key (To Your Heart) - 4 - 2

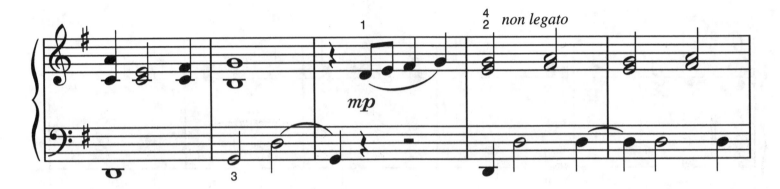

Coda

cresc.

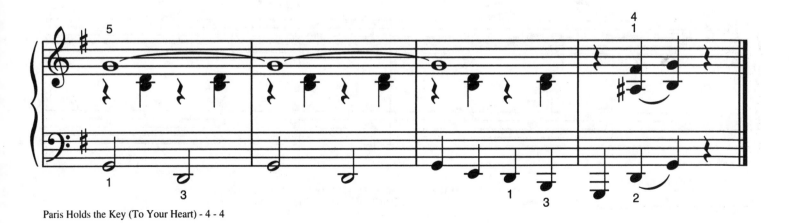

Paris Holds the Key (To Your Heart) - 4 - 4

From the Twentieth Century Fox Animated Motion Picture "ANASTASIA"

IN THE DARK OF THE NIGHT

Lyrics by
LYNN AHRENS

Music by
STEPHEN FLAHERTY
Arranged by ROBERT SCHULTZ

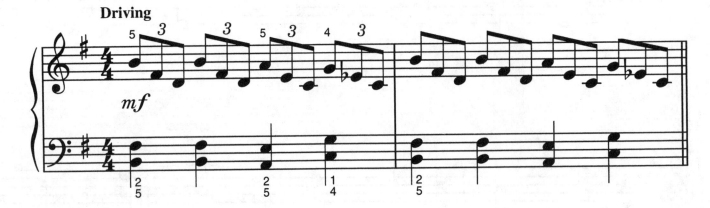

In the Dark of the Night - 5 - 1
AS006

In the Dark of the Night - 5 - 2

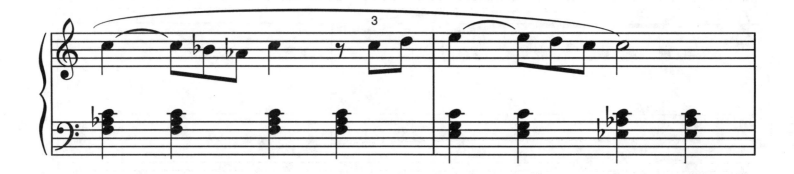

In the Dark of the Night - 5 - 3

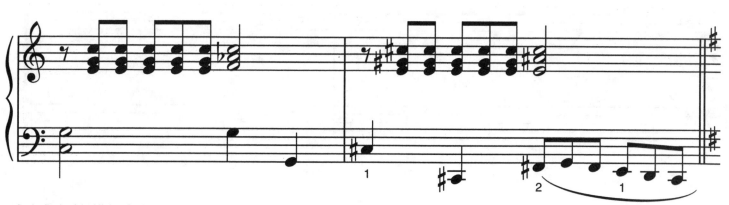

From the Broadway Musical "FIDDLER ON THE ROOF"

MATCHMAKER

Lyrics by
SHELDON HARNICK

Music by
JERRY BOCK
Arranged by ROBERT SCHULTZ

Bright waltz

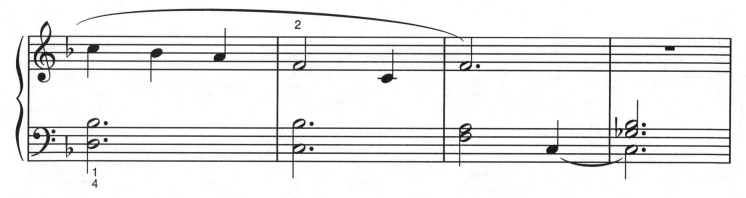

Matchmaker - 3 - 1
AS006

118

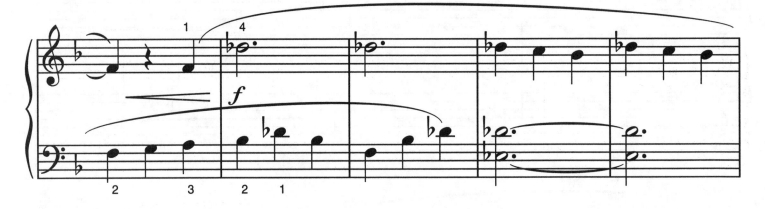

Matchmaker - 3 - 2

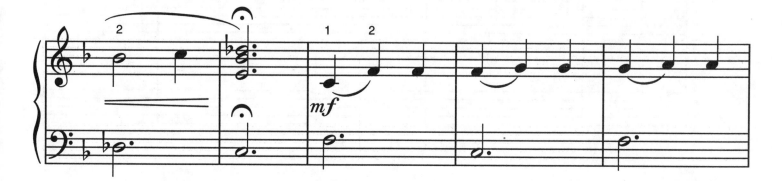

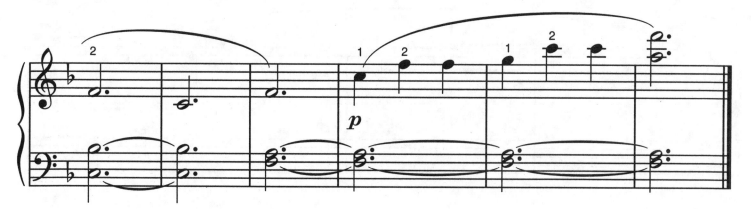

From the Broadway Musical "FIDDLER ON THE ROOF"

TRADITION

Lyrics by
SHELDON HARNICK

Music by
JERRY BOCK
Arranged by ROBERT SCHULTZ

Tradition - 8 - 1
AS006

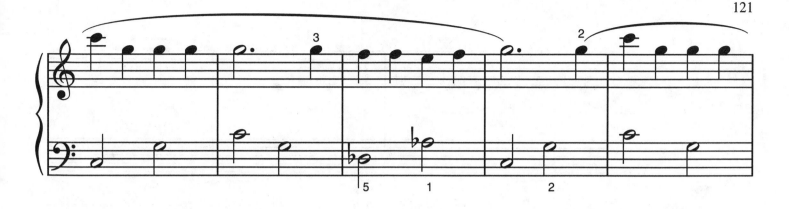

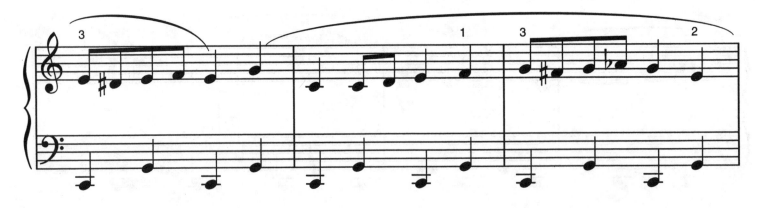

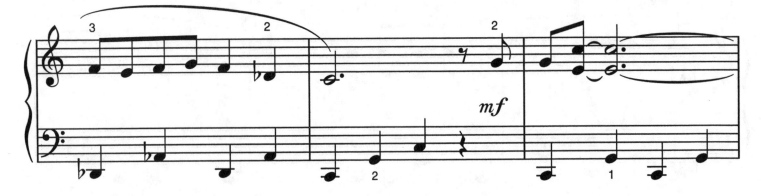

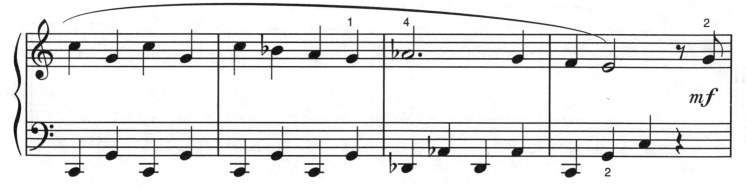

Tradition - 8 - 6

126

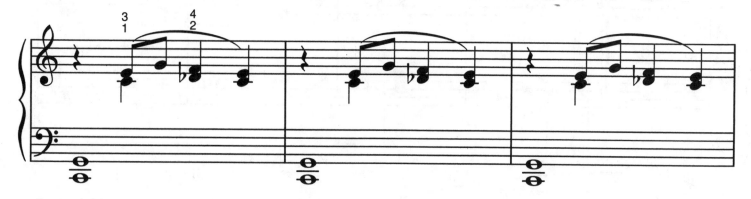

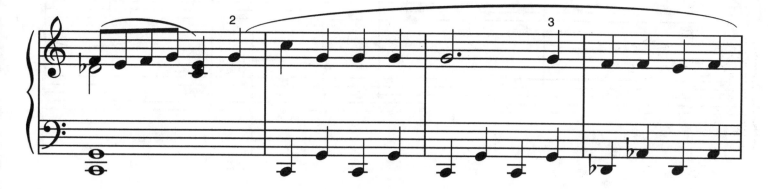

From the Broadway Musical "FIDDLER ON THE ROOF"

TO LIFE

Lyrics by
SHELDON HARNICK

Music by
JERRY BOCK
Arranged by ROBERT SCHULTZ

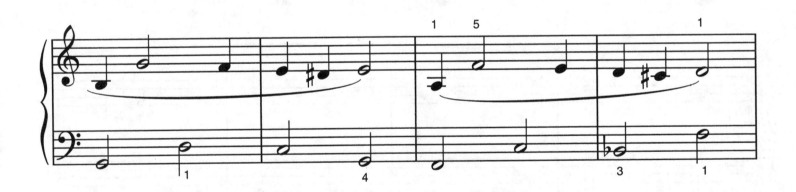

To Life - 4 - 1
AS006

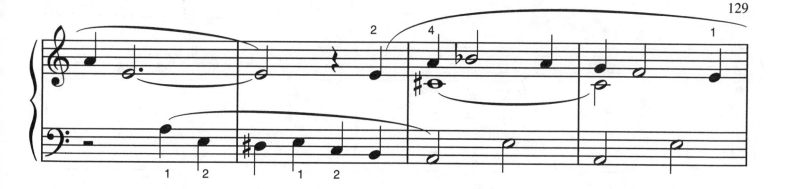

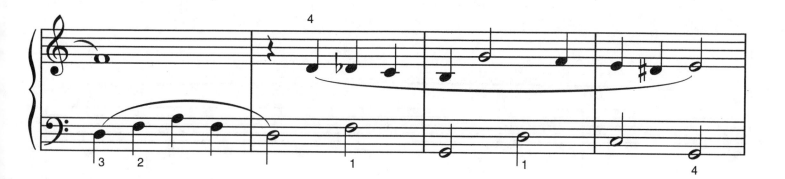

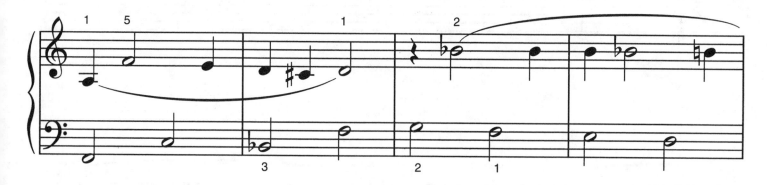

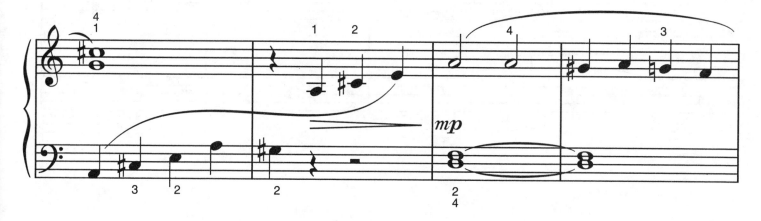

To Life - 4 - 2

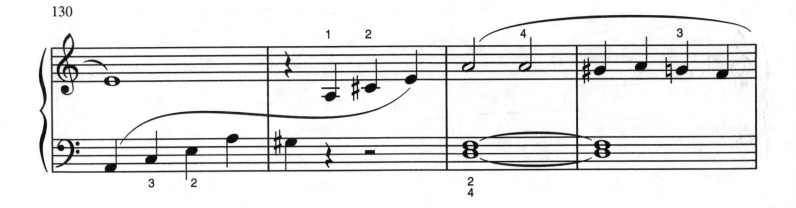

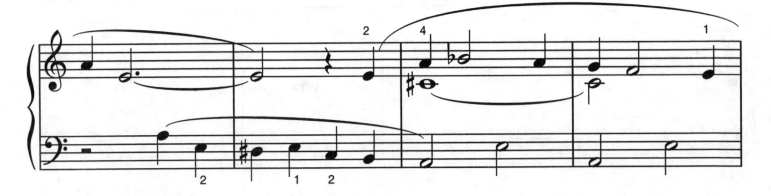

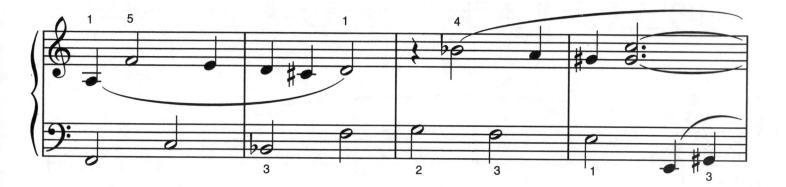

To Life - 4 - 4

From the Broadway Musical "FIDDLER ON THE ROOF"

SUNRISE, SUNSET

Lyrics by
SHELDON HARNICK

Music by
JERRY BOCK
Arranged by ROBERT SCHULTZ

Andantino

Sunrise, Sunset - 4 - 1
AS006

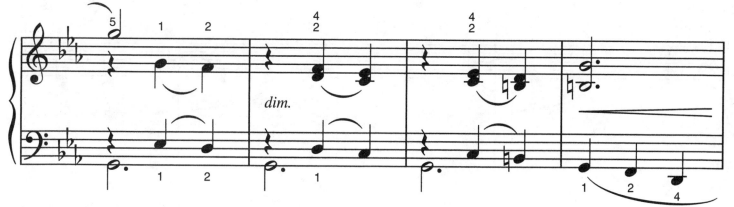

Sunrise, Sunset - 4 - 2

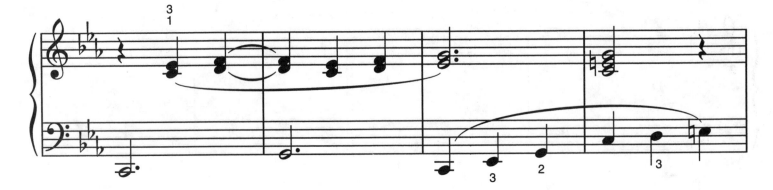

Sunrise, Sunset - 4 - 3

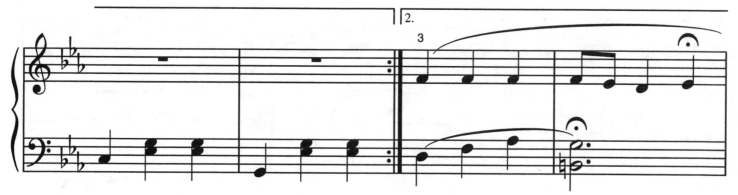

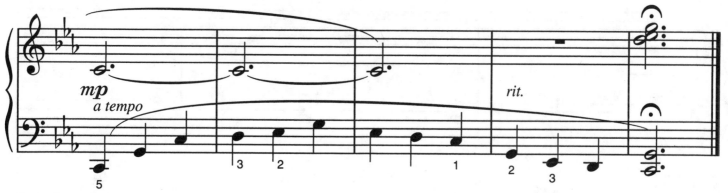

Sunrise, Sunset - 4 - 4

From the Broadway Musical "FIDDLER ON THE ROOF"

SABBATH PRAYER

Lyrics by
SHELDON HARNICK

Music by
JERRY BOCK
Arranged by ROBERT SCHULTZ

Moderately slow, reverently

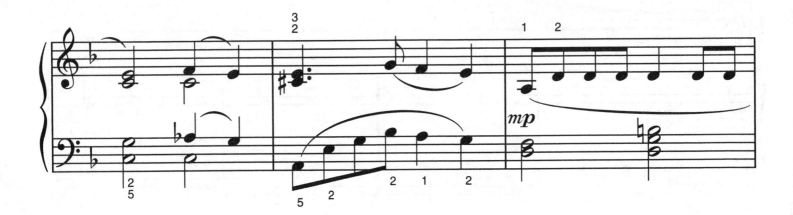

Sabbath Prayer - 3 - 1
AS006

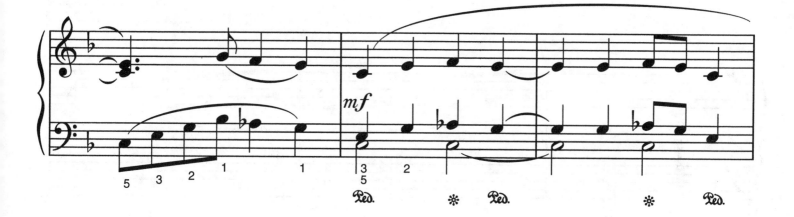

DON'T IT MAKE MY BROWN EYES BLUE

Words and Music by
RICHARD LEIGH
Arranged by ROBERT SCHULTZ

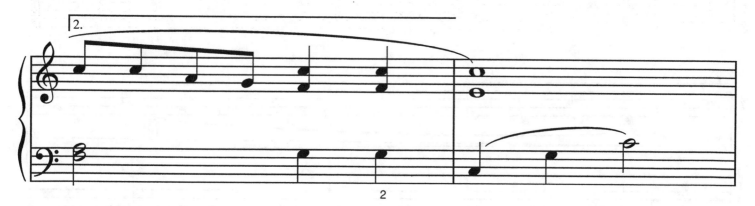

Don't It Make My Brown Eyes Blue - 3 - 1
AS006

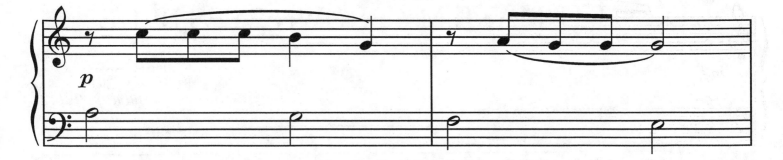

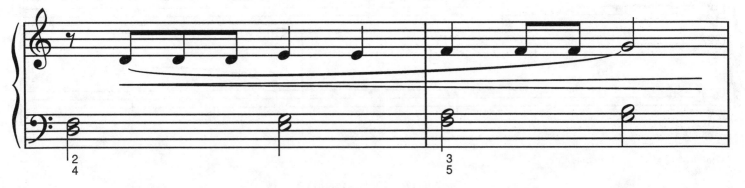

Don't It Make My Brown Eyes Blue - 3 - 2

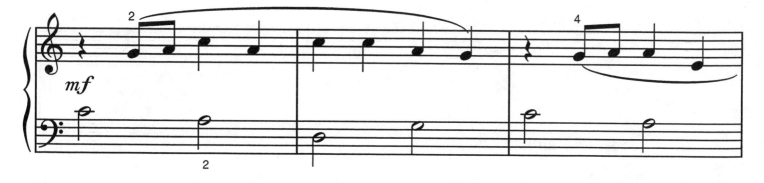

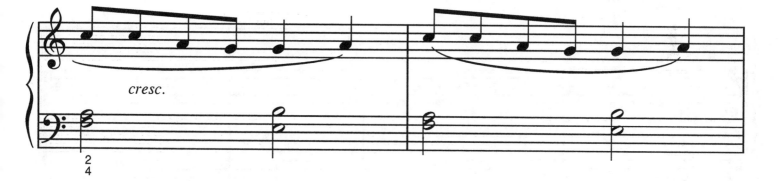

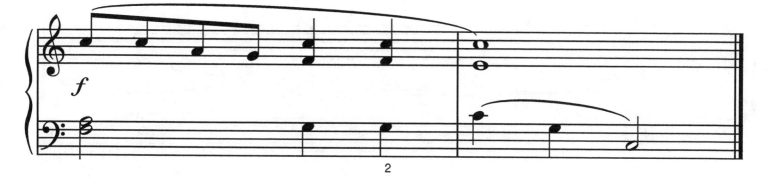

Don't It Make My Brown Eyes Blue - 3 - 3

HEY! BABY!

Words and Music by
MARGARET COBB and
BRUCE CHANNEL
Arranged by ROBERT SCHULTZ

Moderate shuffle

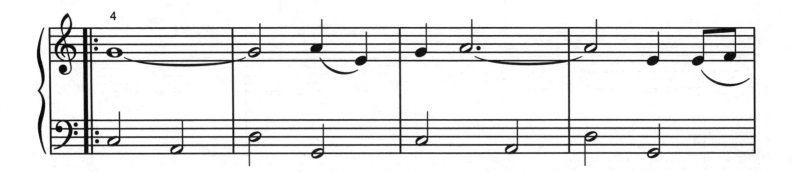

Hey! Baby! - 2 - 1
AS006

THE HOUSE OF THE RISING SUN

Words and Music by
ALAN PRICE
Arranged by ROBERT SCHULTZ

OLD TIME ROCK & ROLL

Words and Music by
GEORGE JACKSON and THOMAS E. JONES III
Arranged by ROBERT SCHULTZ

AS006

THE LION SLEEPS TONIGHT

New Lyric and Revised Music by
GEORGE DAVID WEISS, HUGO PERETTI
and LUIGI CREATORE
Arranged by ROBERT SCHULTZ

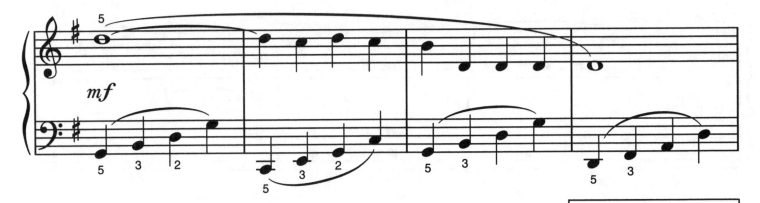

The Lion Sleeps Tonight - 2 - 1
AS006

Slower (even ♪)

The Lion Sleeps Tonight - 2 - 2

MUSTANG SALLY

By BONNY RICE
Arranged by ROBERT SCHULTZ

Very steady ♩ = 100

Mustang Sally - 2 - 1
AS006

(SHE'S) SOME KIND OF WONDERFUL
a/k/a SOME KIND OF WONDERFUL

Words and Music by
J. ELLISON
Arranged by ROBERT SCHULTZ

Moderate rock

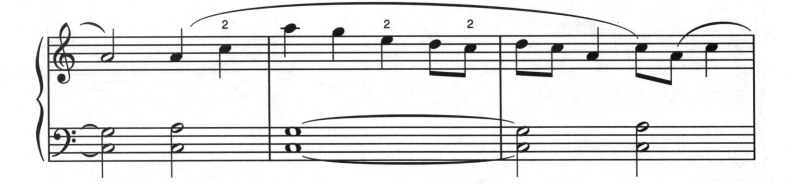

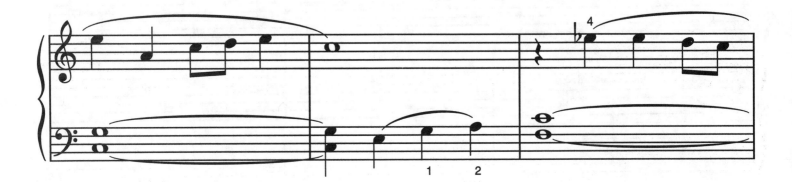

(She's) Some Kind of Wonderful - 2 - 1
AS006

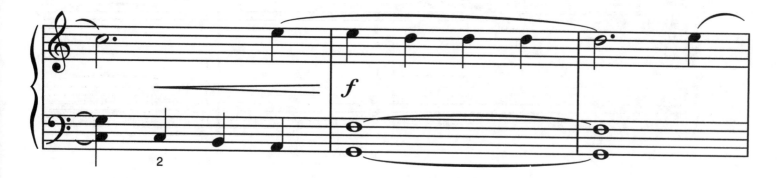

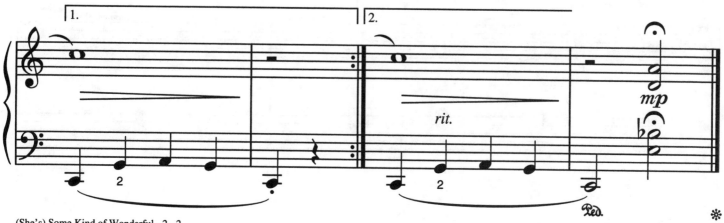

(She's) Some Kind of Wonderful - 2 - 2

WE'VE ONLY JUST BEGUN

Words by
PAUL WILLIAMS

Music by
ROGER NICHOLS
Arranged by ROBERT SCHULTZ

We've Only Just Begun - 2 - 1
AS006

We've Only Just Begun - 2 - 2

SUNNY

Words and Music by
BOBBY HEBB
Arranged by ROBERT SCHULTZ

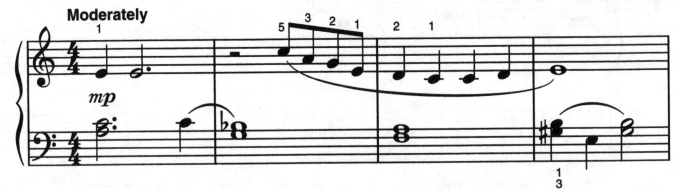

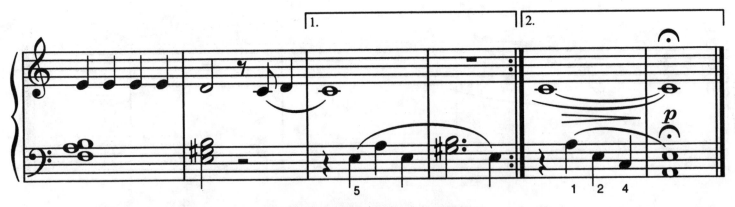

DID YOU EVER SEE A LASSIE?

SINGING GAME
Arranged by ROBERT SCHULTZ

Playfully

GREENSLEEVES

TRADITIONAL ENGLISH
Arranged by ROBERT SCHULTZ

Moderately flowing

Greensleeves - 2 - 1

Greensleeves - 2 - 2

HOME ON THE RANGE

TRADITIONAL
Arranged by ROBERT SCHULTZ

LONDON BRIDGE

SINGING GAME
Arranged by ROBERT SCHULTZ

Playfully

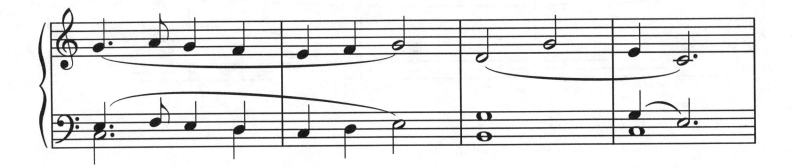

MARY HAD A LITTLE LAMB

TRADITIONAL NURSERY SONG
Arranged by ROBERT SCHULTZ

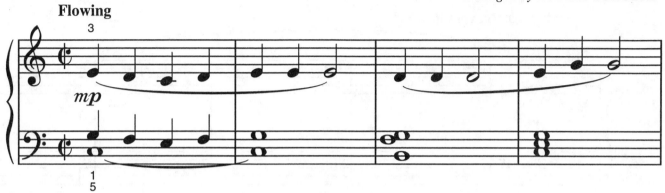

MY BONNIE LIES OVER THE OCEAN

TRADITIONAL
Arranged by ROBERT SCHULTZ

Moderately, very flowing

My Bonnie Lies Over the Ocean - 2 - 1

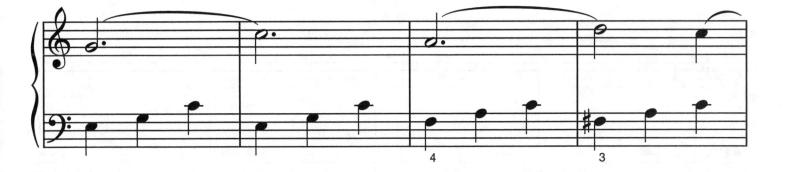

My Bonnie Lies Over the Ocean - 2 - 2

THE PAWPAW PATCH

TRADITIONAL
Arranged by ROBERT SCHULTZ

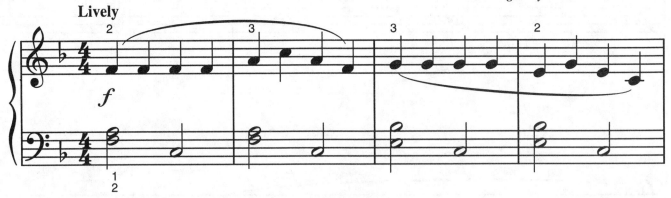

ROCK-A-BYE BABY

TRADITIONAL
Arranged by ROBERT SCHULTZ

Very gently

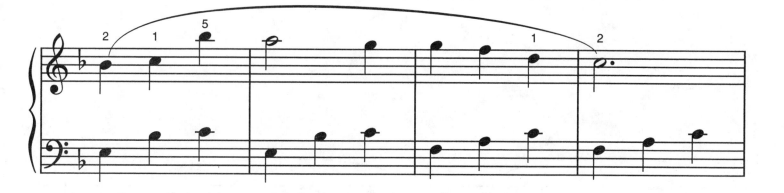

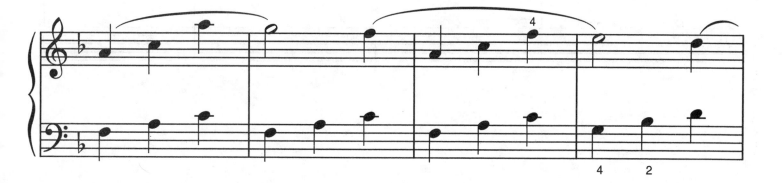

SHENANDOAH

TRADITIONAL
Arranged by ROBERT SCHULTZ

YANKEE DOODLE

TRADITIONAL
Arranged by ROBERT SCHULTZ

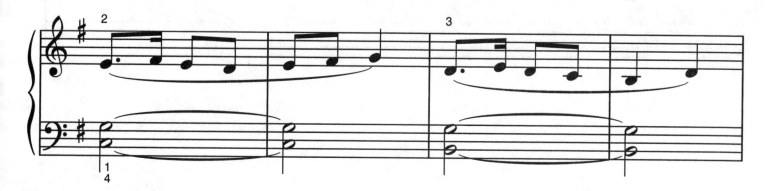

WAYFARING STRANGER

TRADITIONAL
Arranged by ROBERT SCHULTZ

Slowly, sadly

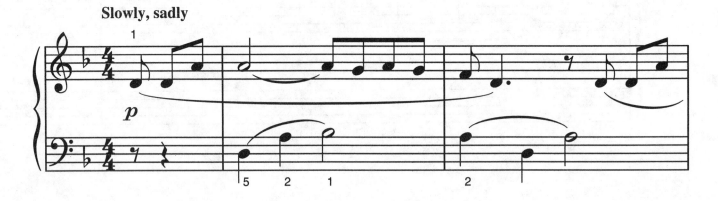

Wayfaring Stranger - 2 - 1

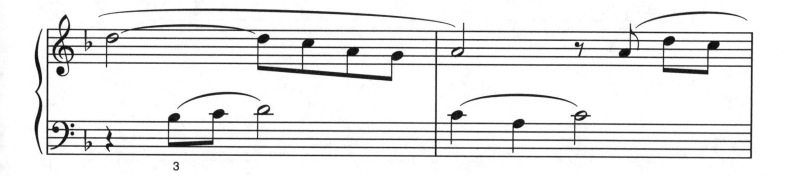

poco rit.

Wayfaring Stranger - 2 - 2

Theme from
THE ANVIL CHORUS
(from the opera *Il Trovatore*)

GIUSEPPE VERDI
Arranged by ROBERT SCHULTZ

Moderato

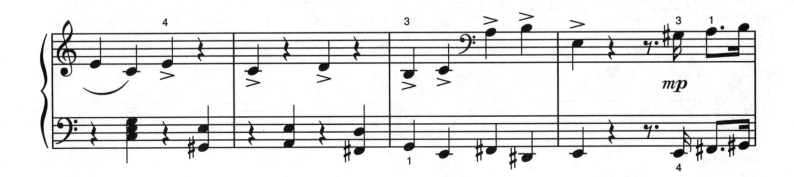

CRADLE SONG
(Wiegenlied)

JOHANNES BRAHMS
Arranged by ROBERT SCHULTZ

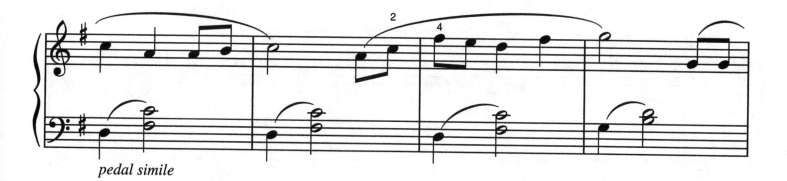

Theme from
BARCAROLLE
(from the opera *The Tales of Hoffmann*)

JACQUES OFFENBACH
Arranged by ROBERT SCHULTZ

Andantino

pedal simile

Theme from Barcarolle - 2 - 1

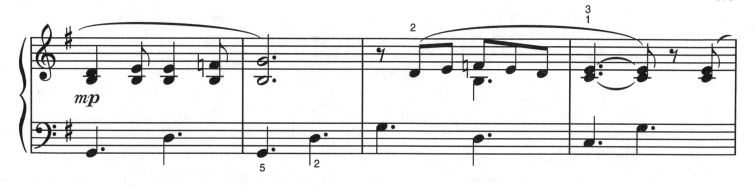

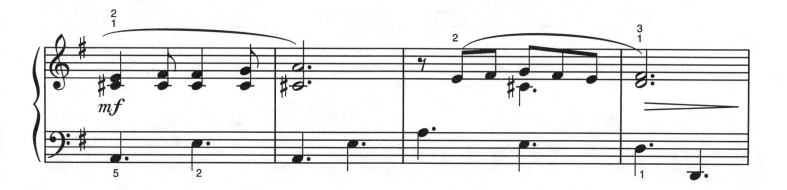

Theme from Barcarolle - 2 - 2

BRIDAL CHORUS
(from the opera *Lohengrin*)

RICHARD WAGNER
Arranged by ROBERT SCHULTZ

Moderato

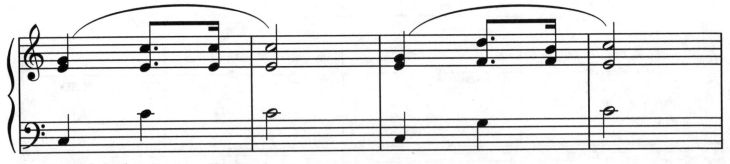

pedal simile

Bridal Chorus - 2 - 1

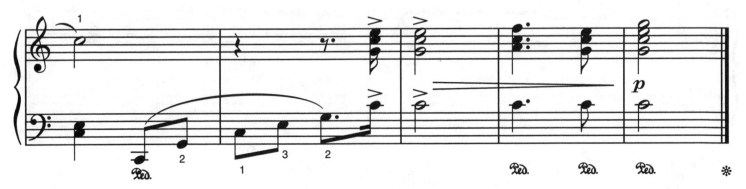

Bridal Chorus - 2 - 2

Theme from
CAN-CAN
(from the operetta *La Vie Parisienne*)

JACQUES OFFENBACH
Arranged by ROBERT SCHULTZ

Allegro con brio

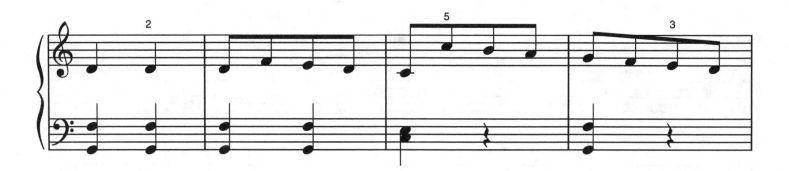

Theme from Can-Can - 2 - 1

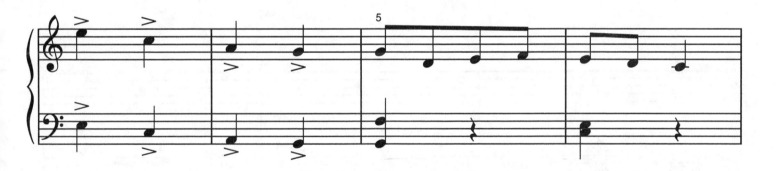

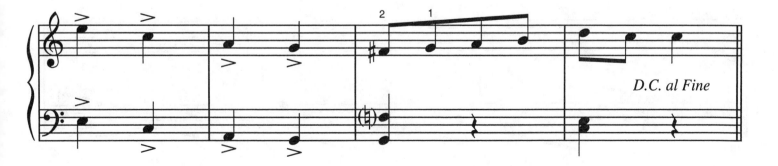

D.C. al Fine

Theme from Can-Can - 2 - 2

Theme from
CANON IN D

JOHANN PACHELBEL
Arranged by ROBERT SCHULTZ

Theme from Canon in D - 2 - 1

Theme from Canon in D - 2 - 2

Theme from
JESU, JOY OF MAN'S DESIRING
(from *Cantata No. 147*)

JOHANN SEBASTIAN BACH
Arranged by ROBERT SCHULTZ

Andante

Theme from Jesu, Joy of Man's Desiring - 2 - 1

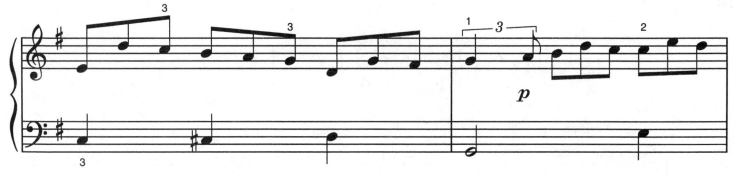

Theme from Jesu, Joy of Man's Desiring - 2 - 2

182

Theme from
LA CI DAREM LA MANO
(from the opera *Don Giovanni*)

WOLFGANG AMADEUS MOZART
Arranged by ROBERT SCHULTZ

Theme from

UN BEL DI

(from the opera *Madama Butterfly*)

GIACOMO PUCCINI
Arranged by ROBERT SCHULTZ

Andante

Theme from
LARGO
(from *The New World Symphony*)

ANTONÍN DVOŘÁK
Arranged by ROBERT SCHULTZ

Largo

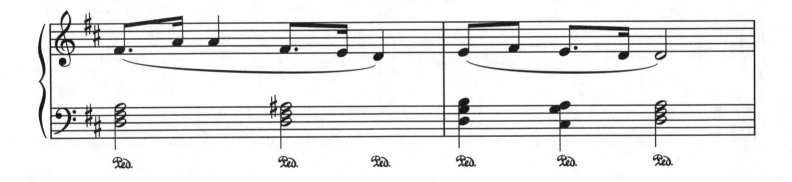

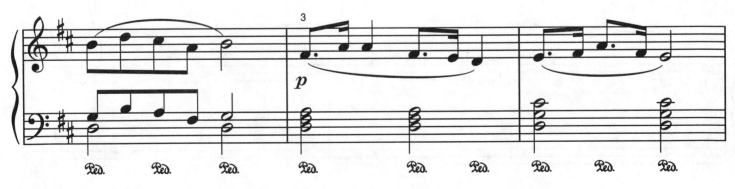

Theme from Largo - 2 - 1

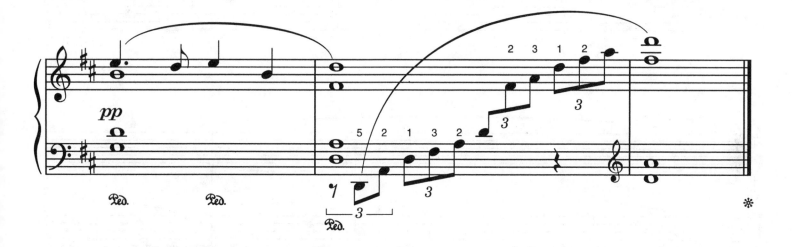

Theme from Largo - 2 - 2

Theme from
THE MERRY WIDOW
(Waltz)

FRANZ LEHAR
Arranged by ROBERT SCHULTZ

Theme from The Merry Widow - 2 - 1

Theme from The Merry Widow - 2 - 2

Theme from
THE SORCERER'S APPRENTICE

PAUL DUKAS
Arranged by ROBERT SCHULTZ

Animato

Theme from The Sorcerer's Apprentice - 2 - 1

Theme from The Sorcerer's Apprentice - 2 - 2

Theme from
SYMPHONY No. 5

LUDWIG VAN BEETHOVEN
Arranged by ROBERT SCHULTZ

Allegro con brio

Theme from Symphony No. 5 - 2 - 1

Theme from Symphony No. 5 - 2 - 2

WALTZ OF THE FLOWERS
(from *The Nutcracker Suite*)

PETER ILYICH TCHAIKOVSKY
Arranged by ROBERT SCHULTZ

Tempo di valse

Waltz of the Flowers - 4 - 1

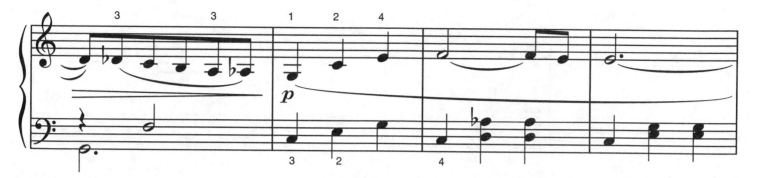

Waltz of the Flowers - 4 - 2

194

Waltz of the Flowers - 4 - 3

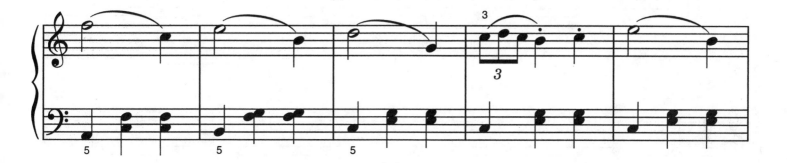

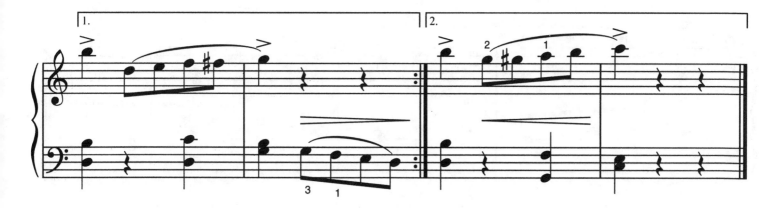

Waltz of the Flowers - 4 - 4

AMERICA
(My Country 'Tis of Thee)

Words by
REV. SAMUEL F. SMITH

Music by
HENRY CAREY
Arranged by ROBERT SCHULTZ

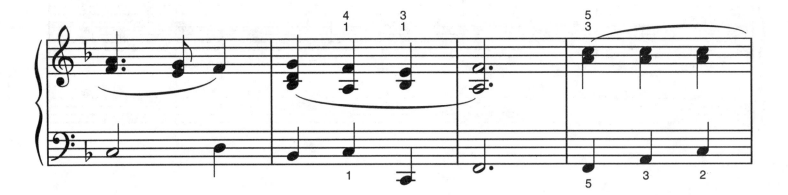

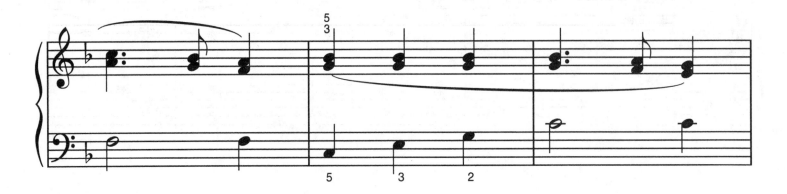

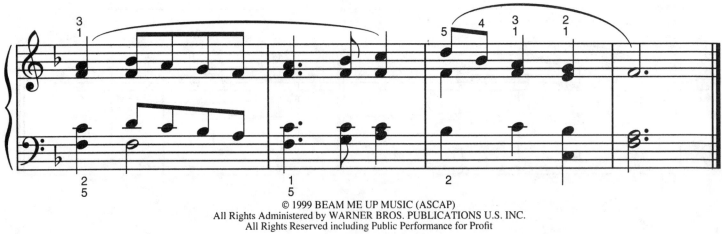

AULD LANG SYNE

TRADITIONAL
Arranged by ROBERT SCHULTZ

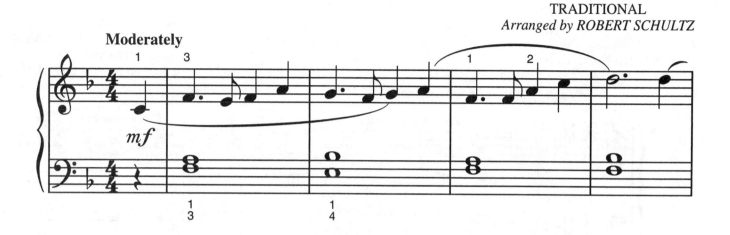

From the Broadway Musical "AIN'T MISBEHAVIN'"

AIN'T MISBEHAVIN'

Words by
ANDY RAZAF

Music by
THOMAS "FATS" WALLER
and HARRY BROOKS
Arranged by ROBERT SCHULTZ

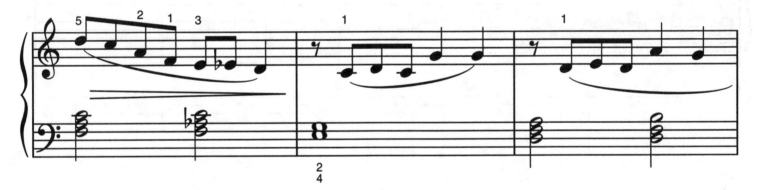

From the Warner Bros. Motion Picture "CASABLANCA"

AS TIME GOES BY

Words and Music by
HERMAN HUPFELD
Arranged by ROBERT SCHULTZ

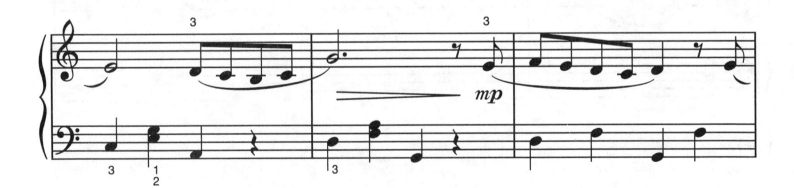

As Time Goes By - 2 - 1
AS006

As Time Goes By - 2 - 2

From the Musical Comedy "SWEET CHARITY"

BIG SPENDER

Music by
CY COLEMAN

Lyric by
DOROTHY FIELDS
Arranged by ROBERT SCHULTZ

Big Spender - 2 - 1
AS006

Big Spender - 2 - 2

Featured in the film "HOLLYWOOD HOTEL" (Warners 1937)

BLUE MOON

By LORENZ HART
and RICHARD RODGERS
Arranged by ROBERT SCHULTZ

Blue Moon - 2 - 1
AS006

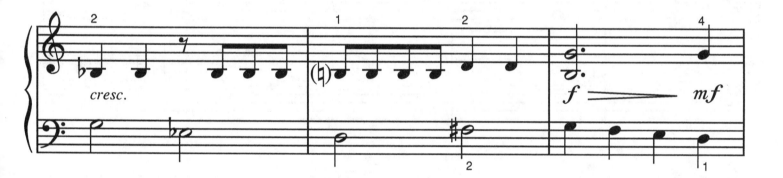

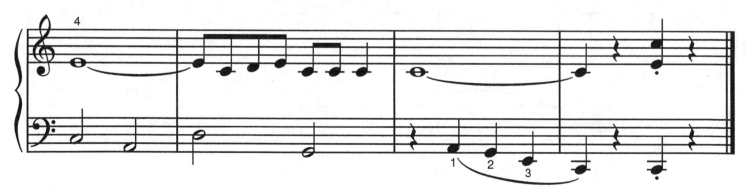

Blue Moon - 2 - 2

Theme Song from the Warner Brothers Production

DEAR HEART

Words by JAY LIVINGSTON and RAY EVANS
Music by HENRY MANCINI
Arranged by ROBERT SCHULTZ

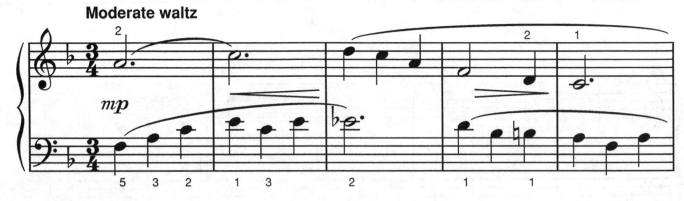

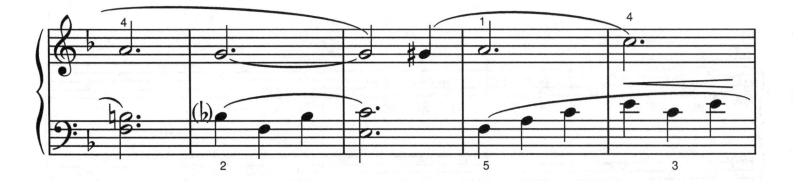

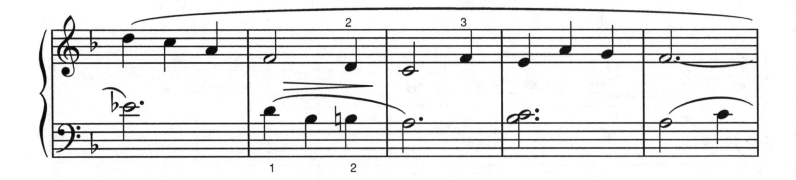

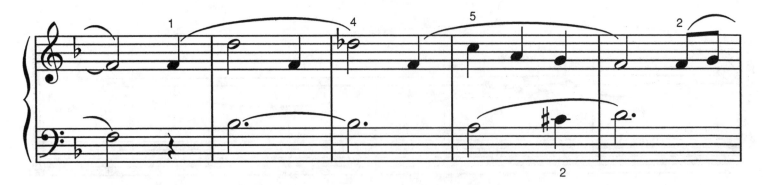

Dear Heart - 2 - 1
AS006

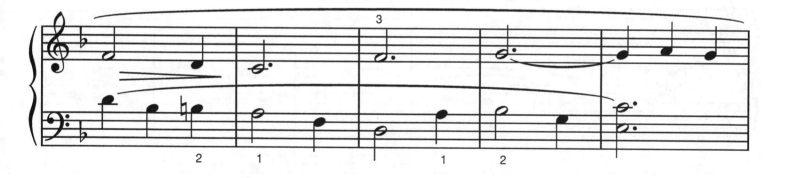

THE ENTERTAINER

By SCOTT JOPLIN
Arranged by ROBERT SCHULTZ

Easy ragtime tempo

From the Motion Picture "MEET ME IN ST. LOUIS"

THE TROLLEY SONG

Lyrics by
HUGH MARTIN

Music by
RALPH BLANE
Arranged by ROBERT SCHULTZ

Bright and lively

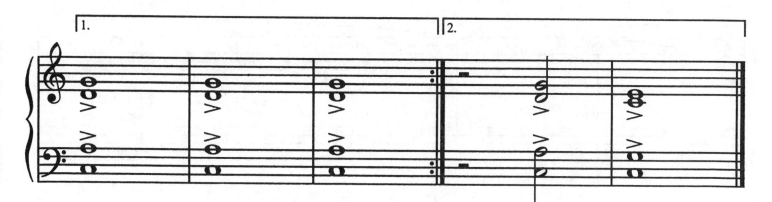

AS006

Introduced by LESLIE CARON and MEL FERRER IN "LILI" (MGM 1953)

HI-LILI, HI-LO

Words by
HELEN DEUTSCH

Music by
BRONISLAU KAPER
Arranged by ROBERT SCHULTZ

Graceful waltz

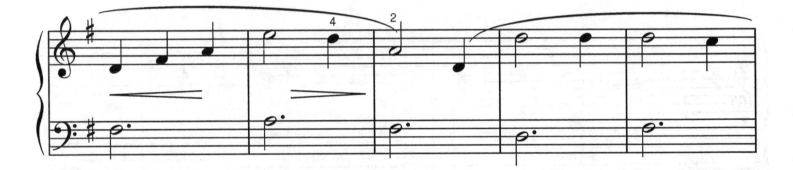

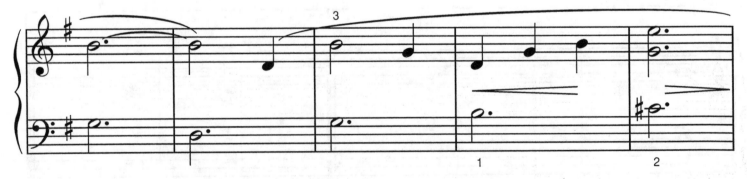

Hi-Lili, Hi-Lo - 2 - 1
AS006

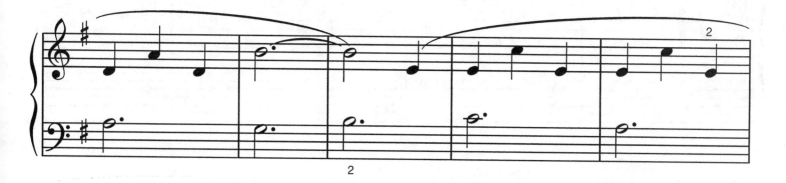

p

Hi-Lili, Hi-Lo - 2 - 2

MY WAY

Original French Words by
GILES THIBAULT

English Words by PAUL ANKA
Music by JACQUES REVAUX
and CLAUDE FRANCOIS
Arranged by ROBERT SCHULTZ

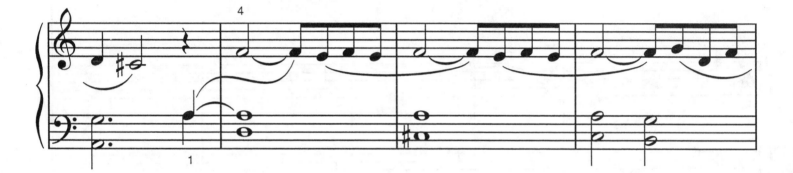

My Way - 2 - 1
AS006

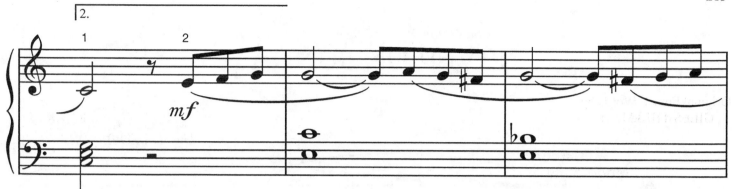

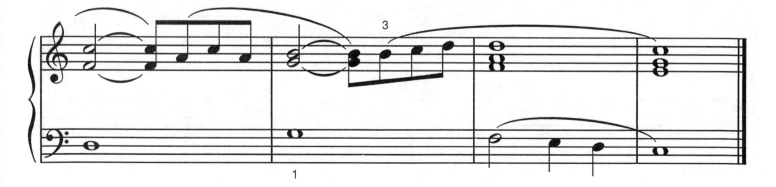

From the Motion Picture "NEVER ON SUNDAY"

NEVER ON SUNDAY

Lyric by
BILLY TOWNE

Music by
MANOS HADJIDAKIS
Arranged by ROBERT SCHULTZ

Never on Sunday - 4 - 1
AS006

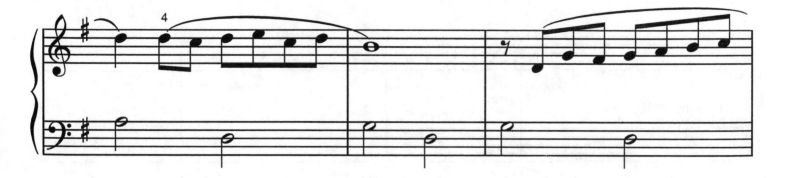

Never on Sunday - 4 - 2

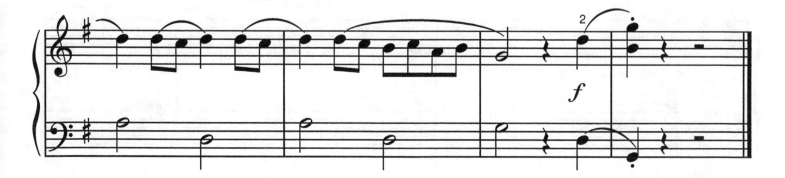

Never on Sunday - 4 - 4

From the Metro-Goldwyn-Mayer Musical Production "SINGIN' IN THE RAIN"

SINGIN' IN THE RAIN

Lyric by
ARTHUR FREED

Music by
NACIO HERB BROWN
Arranged by ROBERT SCHULTZ

Singin' in the Rain - 2 - 1
AS006

219

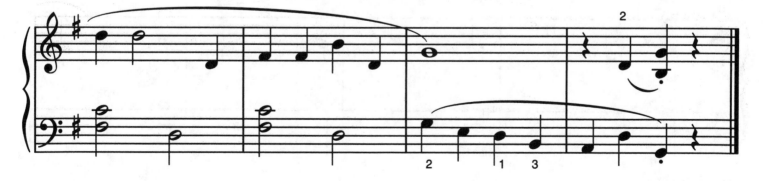

Singin' in the Rain - 2 - 2

From the Warner Brothers Production "THE GREAT RACE"

THE SWEETHEART TREE

Words by
JOHNNY MERCER

Music by
HENRY MANCINI
Arranged by ROBERT SCHULTZ

The Sweetheart Tree - 2 - 1
AS006

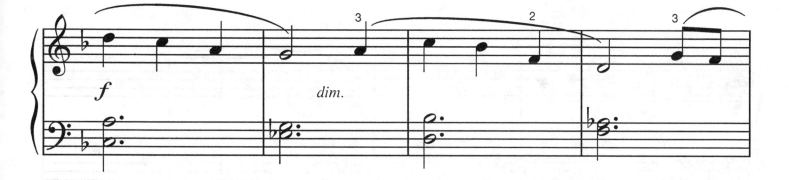

The Sweetheart Tree - 2 - 2

Theme melody from the 20th Century-Fox CinemaScope Production "THREE COINS IN THE FOUNTAIN"

THREE COINS IN THE FOUNTAIN

Words by
SAMMY CAHN

Music by
JULE STYNE
Arranged by ROBERT SCHULTZ

Delicately

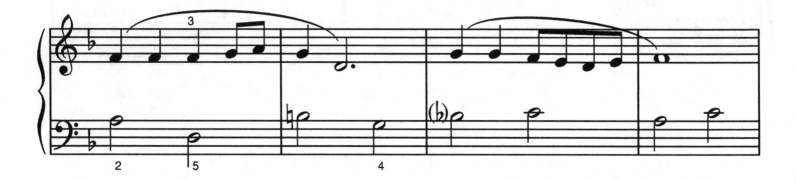

Three Coins in the Fountain - 2 - 1
AS006

ALPHABETICAL INDEX